Praise for *Your Life Is a Story*

"Chesterton famously telegraphed his wife, 'Am in Market Harborough. Where ought I to be?' She replied, 'Home.' Their exchange neatly encapsulates the paradox of human freedom and human destiny, of subjective lives lived within an objective reality. Brady Stiller unpacks this paradox with clarity and insight. In true Chestertonian fashion, he makes a case that is at once simple and profound."

—**Michael Ward**, University of Oxford, author of *After Humanity: A Guide to C.S. Lewis's "The Abolition of Man"*

"If one wants help with the paradox of freedom, one will do well to turn to the master of paradox himself, G.K. Chesterton. This is what Stiller has made possible for us. We see Chesterton's genius through Stiller's thoughtful, insightful, and penetrating treatment."

—**David W. Fagerberg**, Professor Emeritus, University of Notre Dame

"As Brady Stiller rightly points out in this wonderful book, 'any worldview that does not ultimately align to reality is bound to crack.' And so, guided by the joyful wisdom of Gilbert Chesterton, he shows us a worldview that will not fail us; one big enough and humble enough to bring us into contact with reality and into communion with the deeper things of God."

—**Duncan Reyburn**, author of *Seeing Things As They Are: G.K. Chesterton and the Drama of Meaning*

YOUR LIFE IS A STORY

YOUR LIFE IS A STORY

G.K. CHESTERTON AND THE
PARADOX OF FREEDOM

BRADY STILLER

FOREWORD BY DALE AHLQUIST

Published by Word on Fire, Elk Grove Village, IL 60007
© 2023 by Word on Fire Catholic Ministries
Printed in the United States of America
All rights reserved

Cover design by Rozann Lee, typesetting by Marlene Burrell,
and interior art direction by Nicolas Fredrickson

Scripture excerpts are from the New Revised Standard Version Bible:
Catholic Edition (copyright © 1989, 1993), used by permission of the
National Council of the Churches of Christ in the United States of America.
All rights reserved worldwide.

First printing, March 2024

ISBN: 978-1-68578-091-3

Library of Congress Control Number: 2023946274

To *Notre Dame*, Our Lady

Contents

Foreword

Dale Ahlquist

President, The Society of Gilbert Keith Chesterton

For the past many years, I've been waiting for someone like Brady Stiller to come along. And then, well, Brady Stiller came along. He turned out to be much better than whoever it was I thought I was waiting for. His résumé far exceeds what I could have dreamed up: Notre Dame valedictorian; double major in biology and theology; senior thesis highlighting G.K. Chesterton; and valedictory address invoking Chesterton. Then he goes to England to immerse himself more deeply into the prophet who is without honor in his own country. And now, he writes a book on Chesterton. One great mind meets another, and one young man makes the old things new again.

I had the privilege of meeting Brady when he was still a student at Notre Dame. He was part of an enthusiastic collection of students and faculty who would gather regularly for scintillating discussion about all things Chesterton. I wondered: How could this be? It had seemed that this prominent Catholic university had all but forgotten Chesterton, who back in 1930 had been invited as guest lecturer for six weeks and was awarded an honorary doctorate. The English writer, who had never seen a football game in his life, happened to be present at the opening of Notre Dame's famous stadium, where he was given a huge ovation. Those cheers had long gone silent.

But it was at Notre Dame where Brady Stiller met G.K. Chesterton over eighty years after the man himself had visited the campus. It was theology professor David Fagerberg who made the introduction, and Chesterton quickly became Brady's favorite author. It was the saneness and the playfulness of Chesterton's writing that captured him. But it was also the case of one integrated thinker encountering another. Chesterton put everything together. By studying both biology and theology, Brady was also putting everything together. Biology is the study of life. It's slippery. Theology is the logic of God. It's dry. But you can't afford to get either of them wrong. To get life wrong could mean death. To get God wrong could mean damnation. But for the past century or so, especially in the academic world, science and religion have kept to their own departments and haven't really been on speaking terms. But along comes Brady Stiller and gets a major in both disciplines. At Notre Dame. And using a writer who is considered neither a theologian nor a scientist, but a journalist, a poet, and a storyteller.

A good story is memorable because the listener can locate himself in the tale. And Brady realized that his own life, his own story, is part of a larger story, written by the Author of life.

The sciences tend to study things objectively, while the humanities tend toward the subjective. The modern philosophers, such as Nietzsche, Sartre, and Foucault, have fed the culture with doubt, not just of God but of any objective truth. The sciences, on the other hand, leave no room for subjectivity. The result is that objectivity and subjectivity are mutually exclusive. The Christian worldview, however, does not see this conflict. It has, says Brady, "a more capacious answer." And G.K. Chesterton conveys it more perfectly and poetically than anyone. He sees that life is a story, and therefore there is a storyteller. But he also sees that life consists of the familiar and the unfamiliar—in other words, the objective and the subjective.

As one who many years ago stumbled through writing a thesis on Chesterton and the concept of paradox, it is rather a thrill to discover decades later that a new student has accomplished the task in stunning style and with greater gravitas—not only because of his credentials but because of his credibility. I've been waiting for Brady Stiller to come along.

Introduction

"I wish to set forth my faith as particularly answering this double spiritual need, the need for that mixture of the familiar and the unfamiliar which Christendom has rightly named romance."[1]

Whether or not we realize it, we all hold particular principles about the meaning of life. Our principles will place us at a certain point on a spectrum of meaning, which ranges from the extreme of pure objectivity to the extreme of pure subjectivity. At one end are the ideas that all meaning is fully determined, our lives are fated to end a certain way, our actions are occurring out of necessity, and free will is illusory. At the other end of the spectrum, no meaning is determined, our lives can have any one of an infinitude of endings where one is no better than another, our actions are a product of chance, and we are free to create our own identity apart from external influences vying to define us. Certain principles along the spectrum can be classified under official terms, such as karma, predestination, fate, chance, flux, determinism, essentialism, existentialism, and relativism. Although we may not describe our personal beliefs under one of these labels, our principles fall somewhere on this spectrum, either at the extremes or at some point in between.

1. G.K. Chesterton, *Orthodoxy* (Park Ridge, IL: Word on Fire Classics, 2017), 2.

This book will present the worldview of G.K. Chesterton (1874–1936)—viewing life as a story—as not simply a metaphor for life but a definitive philosophical position that occupies a peculiar place on this spectrum of meaning. Making a particularly Chestertonian move, this worldview is best understood as a *paradox*, which for Chesterton is a coexisting of two extremes at their full strength at the same time. As a paradox, this worldview occupies *both* extremes of the spectrum of meaning, cultivating the determinedness and un-determinedness of life that best explains this reality. To claim that life is wholly predetermined would be too simplistic of an explanation for this existence, just as would be the claim that all is flux, chance, or subjective experience. Nor is life's meaning a compromise or a meeting-in-the-middle of the two extremes that would dilute their potency. Rather, life's meaning consists of both extremes at the top of their strength, as Chesterton's notion of paradox evinces. Seen through this lens, this paradoxical position reveals ontological and cosmological truths about meaning, our relatedness to one another, our role in the universe, and the connectedness of all the details comprising the story of existence.

"Meaning" and "freedom" are intrinsically related, and to the extent that they will be key focuses of this book, it is essential to provide up front an operative understanding of these terms and their relationship. Bishop Robert Barron defines freedom, in its highest and most authentic form, as "the disciplining of desire so as to make the achievement of the good first possible, then effortless."[2] As will be seen, Chesterton, too, understands freedom to be inherently conditioned and limited as well as ordered toward achieving the good. Moreover, Bishop Barron defines a meaningful life as "one that is lived in a purposive relationship to values," offering such examples of values as the

---

2. Robert Barron, "The Glory of God Is a Human Being 'Fully Alive,'" Word on Fire, January 22, 2006, https://www.wordonfire.org/articles/barron/the-glory-of-god-is-a-human-being-fully-alive/.

three transcendental properties of being—goodness, truth, and beauty.[3] Chesterton's equivalent is his emphasis on seeing the world aright; one's worldview is indicative of that person's purposive (or lack thereof) relationship to values. For Chesterton, having a healthy worldview (using Bishop Barron's terminology, to be in purposive relationship to values) produces joy, the result of being rightly ordered and a mark of ontological fulfillment, which can be experienced only in part during this life. Based on these definitions, freedom and meaning are related in this way, as will be further explored: freedom is the capacity to subjectively order the materials of this life to objective values, that is, to order life in a meaningful way. Of course, the major philosophical worldviews that Chesterton argued against and the culture of our day do not operate within these same understandings of freedom and meaning, which makes it all the more important to consider Chesterton's worldview in light of postmodern philosophical principles.

Chesterton's worldview can be largely represented by two words, romance and story, both of which characterize Chesterton's paradoxical defense of the objective and the subjective. For Chesterton, romance is adventure, fighting and loving, chivalry, and thrift. Each of these romantic expressions acknowledges both the determinedness and un-determinedness of life. For instance, thrift acknowledges the inherent limits of life, which in turn equips us to use our freedom more effectively and properly within these limits. Moreover, story conveys intentional design, proportion, and various possibilities for a story's ending. Just as with romance, story conveys both determinedness and un-determinedness in life; while our story *may* end in any way, it *should not* end in any way, and we possess the freedom to direct our lives toward an objectively noble ending.

3. "S4: E60—The 4 Horsemen of Meaning | Bishop Barron, John Vervaeke, and Jonathan Pageau," *Jordan B. Peterson Podcast*, September 10, 2021, https://www.jordan bpeterson.com/podcast/s4e60/.

3

Insofar as this book engages Chesterton's worldview, it would seem most appropriate to engage the whole corpus of Chesterton's writings. Like many things about Chesterton, the man is too large to contain and to categorize. While it is true that he was a journalist, this label would be too limiting. He was an author, poet, playwright, novelist, artist, defender of common sense, apologist, philosopher, commentator, and patriotic Englishman. Not only is Chesterton many things, but his corpus is expansive in its volume and extensive in its genres, and its genres cross over into one another's realms, where his philosophical exposition may appear in the middle of a literary critique. Additionally, the reader tends to get the full Chesterton in any of his writings, where even in a biography of Thomas Aquinas or a literary critique of Charles Dickens you may feel you are learning more about Chesterton than the figure he is writing about. As a result, Chesterton's worldview is on full display in any and every genre, from his apologetical books like *Orthodoxy* and *The Everlasting Man* to a daily newspaper column on the Boer War.

Even if one had the time to scour every page of Chesterton's writings, it would not be necessary to arrive at the essence of Chesterton's worldview, which is more extensive and explicit in some works than others. For that reason, those key works of Chesterton's will comprise the scope of this book. *Orthodoxy* will be a central text for several reasons. Chesterton sets out his purpose in *Orthodoxy* as summarizing his worldview in direct response to Mr. G.S. Street, who challenged Chesterton to give an account of his view of the world. Moreover, as Chesterton names in the first chapter as a core purpose of that text, he seeks to convey his worldview as ultimately satisfying the "double spiritual need" of life, what he calls the need for the "familiar and the unfamiliar."[4] An accounting of the familiar and the unfamiliar—the objective and the subjective, the determined

4. Chesterton, *Orthodoxy*, 2.

4

and the undetermined—is the core purpose of this present book, just as it was of Chesterton's *Orthodoxy*. Additionally, Chesterton summarizes his view of life as a story most explicitly within *Orthodoxy*, claiming, "I had always felt life first as a story: and if there is a story there is a story-teller."[5]

In addition to Chesterton's great work *Orthodoxy*, *The Everlasting Man*, which many argue is Chesterton's best book, will be important for understanding Chesterton's worldview. In *The Everlasting Man*, Chesterton offers a perceptive account of two stories that have lost their significance in contemporary society because of dull scientific and reductionist accountings—the story of human history and the story of Christ. As it relates to *Orthodoxy* and Chesterton's view of life as a story, *The Everlasting Man* makes sense of the shape and dramatic trajectory of these stories, revealing further how each of our lives is a story and that our stories fit into a much larger story spanning space and time.

Other prominent writings of Chesterton will be considered as they build upon the core principles of Chesterton's worldview that are on clear display in *Orthodoxy* and *The Everlasting Man*. *Heretics*, *The Thing: Why I am a Catholic*, *The Well and the Shallows*, *What's Wrong with the World*, and Chesterton's autobiography offer illustrative selections consistent with the aforementioned writings. In terms of Chesterton's fictional titles, two will be considered due to their symbolic representation of Chesterton's view of the determined and undetermined—the play *The Surprise* and the novel *The Man Who Was Thursday*. These nonfictional and fictional works, among a few others, paint a clear and comprehensive picture of Chesterton's view of life as a story and the philosophical principles it upholds.

This book contains two parts. Part 1 establishes that Chesterton views life as a story and that this worldview is a definitive philosophical position on meaning and human freedom, while

5. Chesterton, 57.

part 2 then considers Chesterton's worldview up against other prominent philosophical positions that differ in their principles on the objectivity and subjectivity of life—namely, determinism, existentialism, skepticism, and nihilism. These four were intentionally chosen, as they were worldviews that Chesterton directly combated in his writings. Chesterton explicitly names determinism, skepticism, and nihilism throughout his writings and identifies their misalignment with reality, particularly reality's meaningfulness and the relationship between meaning and human freedom. While existentialism is a term that did not arise until the mid-twentieth century, the philosophical position no doubt existed during Chesterton's time, and Chesterton wrote vehemently and extensively against such subjectivist strains in the culture of his day. Against these worldviews, which each provide a limited and unsatisfactory accounting for the objectivity and subjectivity of life, Chesterton's worldview proposes a more capacious position that says yes to both extremes: "Could life's meaning in fact be very objective and very subjective at the same time, and would that not be most true to reality?"

PART I

Your Life Is a Story

THE CHRISTIAN WORLDVIEW AND
THE PARADOX OF FREEDOM

CHAPTER I

Your Life Is a Story

The Worldview of G.K. Chesterton

"I had always felt life first as a story: and if there is a story there is a story-teller."[1]

WORLDVIEWS

It would not take an empirical study canvassing the entire human population to soundly conclude that there are as many ways of seeing the world as there are people alive. One will observe very early on in life that his worldview is shaped by every subjective human experience—being born to a certain set of parents in a certain time in history and particular geographical location, developing thoughts and opinions through every sensory and cognitive experience, and growing up and experiencing this existence from the viewpoint of an unrepeatable identity. In other words, the evidence is endless to defend a subjective experience of the world. From his epistemological journey of coming to know things the way he does, to his unique ontological identity that no other human can embody, to his cosmological perceptions of how everything in the world fits together, a person's experience of reality is remarkably one of a kind.

At the same time, and not in contradiction to subjective experience, worldviews tend to fall into groupings of major philosophical positions along epistemological, ontological, and

1. G.K. Chesterton, *Orthodoxy* (Park Ridge, IL: Word on Fire Classics, 2017), 57.

cosmological lines. For instance, one person may believe that many events occur by fate while another scientifically minded person believes that events are predetermined by subatomic forces and the laws of nature that govern them, but what unites these two different positions is the common thread of determinism. The same holds for the opposite side of the spectrum, with one person holding a relativistic view of morality and the other perceiving events as happening by chance—these are united in their subjectivism.

Now, there is a tendency in our postmodern culture to treat each person's opinions, positions, and worldview as inviolable and deeply personal. Worldviews are a deeply personal matter, but they are not inviolable insofar as they fall into a major philosophical grouping, with one philosophical position vying to be more right and true to reality than other worldviews on offer. These major philosophical positions—whether determinism, subjectivism, skepticism, or nihilism—are all contending to be the most valid way of viewing the world, and the thinkers who defend them are not in the business of respecting other major philosophical positions. Even the avid subjectivist, at the risk of contradicting his own commitment to subjectivism, would fight to the death asserting that subjectivism is the worldview every person should hold, an ironically objective claim nonetheless. From the perspective of these larger camps, these philosophical worldviews are mutually exclusive; their tenets exclude belonging to multiple camps. One cannot be a committed determinist and an enduring existentialist and a steadfast skeptic at the same time, because each philosophical position has tenets that directly contradict those of the others.

If everyone's view of the world is unique, yet everyone's worldview on freedom and meaning tends to fall into a larger philosophical camp that makes a fierce claim about being the most correct view of reality, then a critical question is raised: Is there a most correct worldview as it relates to what is objective and what is subjective in life, and if so, what could it be? To answer this question is the chief interest and purpose of this book.

To make an attempt to answer this central question, it seems most fitting that we would turn to a particular figure for whom worldviews were of supreme interest, particularly because one's worldview not only impacts every choice throughout one's life but also most directly determines one's happiness. As this figure himself claims, "But there are some people, nevertheless—and I am one of them—who think that the most practical and important thing about a man is still his view of the universe."[2] For G.K. Chesterton (1874–1936), one's worldview was all it took to figure out everything about a man. He had an uncanny ability to diagnose the worldviews of those around him, not only tracing people's positions back to the root causes to explain why they believed what they did but also possessing the foresight to predict what choices people's worldviews would lead them to make, as well as identifying the ultimate prognosis of their worldviews. While Chesterton did treat the worldviews of fellow writers and public figures—such as Joseph McCabe or Bernard Shaw, whose worldviews he wrote about at length—as their own deeply held beliefs, that did not prevent him from categorizing their worldviews based on their alignment to major philosophical positions. For Chesterton, people's worldviews really do follow patterns, to the point that so-called "new" philosophical movements during his time were really just new emphases on ancient principles already explored and tested over the ages. We could imagine Chesterton agreeing with Alfred North Whitehead (1861–1947), who famously claimed that the European philosophical tradition "consists of a series of footnotes to Plato."[3]

This leads us to make the same demand of Chesterton as Mr. G.S. Street made of him. If Chesterton has the right to

2. G.K. Chesterton, *Heretics*, in *The Collected Works*, 1:41.

3. Alfred North Whitehead, *Process and Reality*, ed. David Ray Griffin and Donald W. Sherburne (New York: The Free Press, 1978), 39.

diagnose and critique the worldviews of prominent figures as flawed, then Chesterton should give us an account of his own worldview and why he believes it is more sound than theirs. Chesterton eagerly took the provocation from Mr. Street, producing the grand apologetical masterpiece *Orthodoxy* (1908) to expound his worldview, which could be summarized thus: far pre-dating his formal adoption of the Catholic Christian faith, Chesterton had always viewed life as a "story," a worldview that he would later discover had already been the Christian worldview for nearly two millennia. Up to that point of publicly expounding his worldview, Chesterton's early life could be characterized as a search for a right worldview that best explains this reality. It never was a question of whether worldviews were a matter of personal taste. Instead, Chesterton had always treated worldviews in relation to an objectively right worldview that—even if he would never come to find it—he was convinced others had already found. And it was in this very way of viewing life as a story that he would find himself unknowingly already within the bounds of Christianity.

In this discussion of philosophical positions contending for the title of "most correct worldview," we might next wonder if Chesterton considered his worldview on the same level as other dominant philosophies making objective claims about reality and asserting their framework as one that all people should be operating within. The short answer is "yes," and to provide the long answer is the purpose of the remainder of this book—to show why Chesterton believed that the view of life as a story (which was not only his own worldview but also that of Christianity) is one that best explains this existence and, therefore, one that all people should hold if they are to discover the key that unlocks the secrets of the world.

Far more than a metaphor or a personal liking, to view life as a story is an audacious and expansive philosophical framework that seeks to explain all things, all peoples, all times, and all places. This position makes fierce epistemological claims about what we can know to be true. It takes a strong ontological position that life has meaning to be discovered, that life has a meaningful trajectory, that the story of life should end a certain way but could nevertheless end in any way as a result of free will, that the story of life has an author embellishing it with choice details, and that the purpose of human beings as protagonists of the story is to overcome the central conflict in pursuit of a noble resolution. Likewise, it proposes cosmological views on the existence of the universe and how human beings fit into this existence, offering a hermeneutical lens through which to make sense of every detail of life. Ultimately, to view life as a story is the position of the Christian tradition, and like any serious philosophical worldview, it seeks to explain everything and to traverse the universe leaving no stone unturned.

Now, if someone who had never read Chesterton's writings had been given one of his books to read—let us say his more well-known books *Orthodoxy* or *The Everlasting Man*—and had to identify three key words that captured the essence of his worldview, those three words would most likely be "story," "romance," and "paradox." These three terms are distinct from each other and have multiple meanings that are core to Chesterton's worldview, but they are also interconnected in their principles. Chesterton perceives life as a story, a story that takes the ideal form and genre of a romance story, and a story that has multiple paradoxes at its core.

To first begin with Chesterton's idea of story, "story" meant many things to Chesterton, all of which he viewed as consistent with Christianity and as best revealing the deepest truths about reality. For Chesterton, a story must have a storyteller to intentionally determine every detail, down to the smallest of details; a story is a work of art with proportion and personal expression; and a story has an ideal ending that it should (with moral and ontological imperative) achieve but is not predetermined to achieve. These principles may seem self-evident, but for Chesterton and for Christians, the application of these principles to reality is of utmost significance, as they comprise the Christian "philosophy," in the sense of a system that seeks to make sense of existence. To offer an initial example, to claim that our lives are stories with a storyteller opens up a whole line of questioning: "Who is the storyteller? Why did the storyteller choose these exact details? What is the ideal ending that the storyteller had in mind?" Someone who believes in a well-meaning storyteller will approach life's meaning very differently from someone else who believes that life is better accounted for as an accidental unfolding of chance events.

As for Chesterton's idea of romance, "romance" is best understood as the ideal "genre" of the story of life. This is opposed to viewing life as a horror story, which would be more in line with how the nihilistic philosophy views the story of life, if nihilism could even be said to call life a story. Love and adventure are at the core of Chesterton's understanding of romance, but lest the concepts of "love" and "adventure" be dismissed as too obvious or even overly sentimental, these concepts carry strong philosophical presuppositions in Chesterton's understanding. For Chesterton, love was less of a delightful emotion and more of a fierce claim about the primitiveness of goodness and that goodness should be defended against the onslaught of opposing forces. This is essentially the Christian understanding of love as "willing the good" of another person, a much stronger treatment of love than reducing love to an emotion. On a similar note, Chesterton's understanding of "adventure" was less about life being fun—though Chesterton did view life as fun. More accurately, claiming that life is an adventure is to make two key inferences about reality: first, that conflict is an inherent part of the human experience and that a sense of adventure arises from the fight to overcome it, and second, that the future is undetermined and offers the exciting opportunity to redirect the story in the right direction. Thus, the principles undergirding Chesterton's idea of story and romance are deeply philosophical in their approach, Christian in their essence, and universal in their applicability.

Having set the context for Chesterton's understanding of world-views and the defining principles of his own worldview, we now consider each of the principles of Chesterton's understanding of "story" and "romance," as well as how they begin to form a system of understanding the world. It makes sense to start from the beginning with Chesterton's earliest intuition about life's meaning, namely, that life is a story with a storyteller, which he put thus: "And this pointed to a profound emotion always present and sub-conscious; . . . I had always felt life first as a story: and if there is a story there is a story-teller."[4] This succinct statement of Chesterton's earliest intuition about life's meaning, one that he would carry with him the rest of his life, is powerful enough to capture nearly all of Chesterton's worldview, and much of the Christian philosophy can be deduced from this single statement.

To begin with the idea of story, understood in the most general sense, a story is a narrative account of a series of events that proceed along an arc, including an opening, the rise of a central conflict, a climax, and a resolution. As will be seen in more detail, Chesterton interprets this story arc as applying not only to each person's life but also to the course of history, which is precisely the Christian position. Each person's life begins with years of childhood innocence followed by the age of reason and the battle against evil forces in preservation of the good. The climax is the realization of one's purpose in life, and the resolution is the fulfillment of the story after death as it finds its place more perfectly among other human stories and God's ultimate story

---

4. Chesterton, *Orthodoxy*, 57.

for existence. This story arc present in each person's life mirrors the greater story of salvation history, which begins when human beings are created by God in a state of innocence and is followed by the fall of humanity, the battle against evil for ages to come, and the climax of God's coming to earth to finally defeat evil. The resolution will be the consummation of the grand story of creation at the end of time.

Moreover, stories can take on any number of genres, such as fantasy, mystery, and horror. This raises questions about what genre or genres Chesterton was referring to when he called life a story. Does each person's story have its own genre? Is there an ideal genre that each person's story should take on? We might also then wonder what genre the story of salvation history is. Fortunately, the answer to all of these questions is very easy to identify from Chesterton's writings and his worldview, because the answer is nearly everywhere he put pen to paper. According to Chesterton, life, when it is lived to its fullest, is best characterized as a *romance* story, which connotes everything from the sensation of love to the thrilling adventure of battle. To offer only one example here, Chesterton finishes his autobiography referring to his own life as a romance story: "I am finishing a story; rounding off what has been to me at least a romance."[5]

Just as important as identifying the genre that life's story should take on—namely, romance—is pointing out the genres that life should not take on. Other philosophies, if they view life as a story at all, may view life as a tragedy or a horror story, wherein one's life is a series of unfortunate events logically tending toward downfall or beset constantly by suffering and negative forces with little hope for a happy ending. Surely, this is the position of the pessimist, who does not stop at complaining about there being too little good in the world but goes so far as to

---

5. G.K. Chesterton, *The Autobiography of G.K. Chesterton*, in *The Collected Works of G.K. Chesterton* (San Francisco: Ignatius, 1988), 16:329–330.

question the value of good itself.[6] Many other philosophies, such as fatalism, do not even grant that life is a story but instead treat life more as a "science or a plan, which must end up in a certain way."[7] Nevertheless, for those who grant that life is a story, the type of genre will impact how every element of the story is interpreted and where the story is headed, whether glory or doom.

Perhaps most obvious, yet most foundational, in Chesterton's understanding of the story of life is that it has a storyteller. Out of this simple truth arises every philosophical implication about design, purpose, meaning, and freedom. On the most basic level, to claim that a story has a storyteller is to attribute every detail of the story, every description of color or environment or personality, to the intentional choice of the author. The point is almost so self-evident that it risks jeopardizing the significance of the claim. To say that there is a personality behind the story is to make a definitive ontological claim that the story has meaning. Applied to the story of life, if God is the storyteller of our lives and the storyteller behind history, then he must be meaning something in the details that he chose, because this existence could have been very different. It means that a purpose underlies everything that has been created, almost literally in the sense that purpose is lying in waiting to be discovered, where "everything has a story tied to its tail."[8] It is likewise a bold claim about the objectivity of meaning that logically results from the choice of the divine storyteller. This flies in the face of popular philosophies and subscribers to those philosophies who, on scientific or philosophical grounds, deny the existence of any objective meaning to be found outside of the relative meaning that individuals create.

6. Chesterton, 104.

7. Chesterton, *Orthodoxy*, 137.

8. Chesterton, 161.

But God is not the only storyteller. We are also the story-tellers. If God is truly free, and if man's freedom is not an illusion but a powerful capacity to effect change upon reality, and if the divine and human freedoms are not mutually exclusive or in competition, then we arrive at the concept of co-creation, whereby both God and man are cooperatively writing the story. Both God and man, through the ordering capacity that is the will, order creation in such a way that it becomes meaningful. This ability to make life meaningful by ordering creation toward objective values is the capacity that God equipped humanity with above all other creatures, by virtue of creating man in his image and likeness. However, unlike God's omnipotent capacity, humanity's capacity to order creation is limited. God's freedom is the capacity to both create from nothing and to order what he created, while man can only order what God has already created. Put another way, God, in his very nature, is the standard of beauty, goodness, and truth, and he orders creation to himself; we do not create these ends, but can use our freedom to order creation toward the reality established by God. This is an inherent limitation to man's ability to create meaning, which is not to render the capacity as ultimately futile—as many other dominant philosophies might conclude. But even those who do not grant the existence of God or the existence of objectively determined meaning must still admit, unlike many resistant postmodern thinkers, that the ability to create meaning has its natural limits within which to operate.

STORY: WORK OF ART

In addition to having a trajectory, a genre, and a storyteller, Chesterton considered a story to be a work of art. As a work of art, a story is an expression of the artistic capacity to create and order details in a way that expresses beauty and truth. According to Chesterton, "Art is the signature of man," a creative capacity that separates mankind from the animal kingdom.[9] Unlike the rest of the animals, man is "a creator as well as a creature. . . . Man is the microcosm; man is the measure of all things; man is the image of God."[10] Implicit in this statement is the claim that art is the signature of God as well, who created mankind in his image and likeness. If God and man are related in this way, it is not a stretch to apply the criteria of human artistic creations to God's creation, which is certainly no less artistic in its expression. Indeed, Chesterton does call God an artist of his creation: "For this world of different and varied beings is especially the world of the Christian Creator; the world of created things, like things made by an artist."[11] Thus, in being the divine storyteller, God also is artist of a masterful creation.

Just as a story is shaped by intentional details of the author, a work of art similarly conveys an intentional act of the will by the artist. The fact that "art is limitation" is "the most decisive example of pure will."[12] Art is a willful limitation in the sense that to draw a particular thing, like a giraffe, the artist is required to draw an animal with a long neck and not a short one.[13] Though there is considerable room for creative license, to deviate from the rules and alter the details in the extreme would be to lose the sense of what the artist wanted to draw in the first place. A paradox though it may be, God made an act of self-limitation in creating a world with very particular proportion, definition, and variety. God "limited" himself—however this may be theologically interpreted—when making the world as it is and not another way; he made a specific choice for how the world would unfold, with certain laws and rules, though God himself is not

9. G.K. Chesterton, *The Everlasting Man*, in *The Everlasting Man: A Guide to G.K. Chesterton's Masterpiece*, ed. Dale Ahlquist (Elk Grove Village, IL: Word on Fire, 2023), 39.

10. Chesterton, 41–42.

11. G.K. Chesterton, *St. Thomas Aquinas*, in *The Collected Works*, 2:538.

12. Chesterton, *Orthodoxy*, 36.

13. Chesterton, 36.

bound by his own created laws.[14] Even in entertaining this idea of God's self-limitation in the act of creating, the creation of the world was also paradoxically an over-flowing of God's love. Creation is both divine thrift and divine overabundance at the same time.

Art is also an expression of will in another sense—the artistic motive is to express a story or to find one already within things. As artist, man feels what Chesterton calls "the ache of the artist," understood to be the longing "to find some sense and some story in the beautiful things he sees; his hunger for secrets and his anger at any tower or tree escaping with its tale untold. He feels that nothing is perfect unless it is personal."[15] Chesterton expresses in an early notebook how the various details of life find their purpose fitting into one's story: "What is the good of all songs, poems, denunciations, schools, ideas, what is the use of any genius, prophet, poet, of any Bible or Church if not as something entering into the plain story of a man's life. A story is the highest work. For the world is a story, every part of it. And there is nothing that can touch the world or any part of it that is not a story."[16] Every detail of life demands explaining; every created thing will not let the human heart rest until it shows its purpose in the big picture or its proportion to everything else. This notion of the ache of the artist seems related to what Chesterton conveys as a tendency toward personification or anthropomorphism of created things.[17] Personification expresses a longing to establish a personal connection with impersonal, inanimate objects. One could say that the Incarnation satisfied a desire to see God in a way that man could relate to. We might wonder if

14. This is a similar principle to how God has ordered the economy of salvation through the sacraments: "God has bound salvation to the sacrament of Baptism, but he himself is not bound by his sacraments" (CCC 1257).

15. Chesterton, *Everlasting Man*, 161.

16. Chesterton, "Ex B-Lib," no. 1EE in GKC Photocopies, GKC Library.

17. Chesterton, *Everlasting Man*, 161.

Chesterton was hinting at the self-limiting act of the Incarnation when suggesting that mankind longs to anthropomorphize the entire universe: "And when the whole universe looks like a man we fall on our faces."[18]

Moreover, if this existence was created by an artist, then the artist must have necessarily made deliberate choices about every detail of its composition. Consistent with the Christian worldview, Chesterton has a providential view of the world, which he believes to have been designed and intelligently wrought together by God: "Proportion cannot be a drift: it is either an accident or a design."[19] Chesterton rules out the former theory that this proportion is an accident because even the smallest details of creation, such as the colors of things, struck him as too deliberate to have been random: "Every colour has in it a bold quality as of choice; the red of garden roses is not only decisive but dramatic, like suddenly spilt blood. He feels that something has been done."[20] Chesterton views God as the artist and creation as an intentional work of art with proportion.

STORY: PROPORTION

So far, we have already seen glimpses of how Chesterton's view of life as a story establishes a position on what is subjective and what is objective. For instance, the divine Author has set an objective order for creation within which humanity, as co-author, has the capacity to subjectively co-create meaning aligned to the objective order. How this worldview fully accounts for the balance of objectivity and subjectivity relative to other philosophical positions is a task for a later chapter, but we are beginning to see how the principles of story set up this framework.

---

18. Chesterton, *Heretics*, 120–121.
19. Chesterton, *Orthodoxy*, 112.
20. Chesterton, 55.

An additional principle that contributes to the objectivity of the story is that of "proportion." As a work of art, a story has proportion, which for Chesterton is an objective arrangement by a personal will and intelligent mind, and it is an inherent property of a story. Stories contain many elements, some objective and others subjective: "A story has proportions, variations, surprises, particular dispositions, which cannot be worked out by rule in the abstract, like a sum."[21] If life is a story, then there is a personal author of this story.[22] And if there is a personal author, then the world may not be tending toward a simple, one-sided objectivity but rather toward a complex, multi-faceted objectivity that only a rational being could create. This "one particular arrangement" of qualities is what Chesterton calls the "proportion" of a story or work of art.[23]

Without a personal will and intellect behind existence, Chesterton supposes that this world would tend toward one simple end, not a complex balance of values and features. Chesterton challenges the conclusion that the world is impersonal simply based on an exact proportion that does not vary. Against the materialist's claim that the world is clockwork because the sun rises without variation, Chesterton suggests that the repetition might be due to an excess, not absence, of life. On the flip side, variation could be due to an absence of life and absence of will.[24] This is all to suggest that the divine will can very well be active in maintaining the objective proportion of this world, while the human will can contribute to subjective variations in the story.

Given the personal will behind the exact proportion of the world, Chesterton suggests that the story of existence would be more satisfying to us if it were to culminate in a particular proportion determined by the divine Author. In Chesterton's

21. Chesterton, *Everlasting Man*, 411.
22. Chesterton, *Orthodoxy*, 57.
23. Chesterton, 112.
24. Chesterton, 56.

theological imagination, the end goal of the story and artwork of creation may very well be a complex, multifaceted picture:

> It must not (if it is to satisfy our souls) be the mere victory of some one thing swallowing up everything else, love or pride or peace or adventure; it must be a definite picture composed of these elements in their best proportion and relation. . . . If the beatification of the world is a mere work of nature, then it must be as simple as the freezing of the world, or the burning up of the world. But if the beatification of the world is not a work of nature but a work of art, then it involves an artist. . . . But only a personal God can possibly be leading you (if, indeed, you are being led) to a city with just streets and architectural proportions, a city in which each of you can contribute exactly the right amount of your own colour to the many coloured coat of Joseph.[25]

This passage begins to offer an understanding of how the subjective elements comprise the objective whole. According to this passage, individuals are their own color—here is the subjective element of the picture. Every person's color is meant to "contribute exactly the right amount"—here is the objective proportion of the picture. As time goes on, the unfinished picture gains more colors and details, but it ought to look a certain way when it is finished at the end of time. The ideal would be for everyone to contribute his or her own color and the right amount of it. However, if some individuals decide to not become part of the picture, the divine artist will have to be creative in making up for the lost colors.

25. Chesterton, 113–114.

STORY: MAY END IN ANY WAY

A final principle of story for consideration, as it relates to Chesterton's understanding of stories and the implications for objectivity and subjectivity, is that a story "may end in any way." In claiming that there is not one inevitable ending of a story, Chesterton is arguing directly against an entirely opposite tendency toward a pure objectivism—viewing an outcome as predestined or necessary due to (or in spite of) preceding events. One such target of Chesterton's argumentation was the Eastern philosophical tradition, which Chesterton knew to differ greatly from Christianity on the notion of inevitability: "To the Buddhist or the eastern fatalist existence is a science or a plan, which must end up in a certain way. But to a Christian existence is a story, which may end up in any way."[26] To assert free will is to sacrifice a single ending—one that could have been objectively best—to an infinitude of endings, because each free action of each free human being will cause a different course of action. This is a common objection against the Christian view of divine freedom and human freedom, that the Christian God would seem to give up an objectively best plan to limited humans by making them free. This dilemma is also at the core of theodicy: "Why would an all-good God allow for evil to exist when the troubled existence that we experience could have been avoided?" This question is not easily answerable, but Chesterton provides a hint at an answer in his play *The Surprise* and his novel *The Man Who Was Thursday*, which we will consider below.

Regarding the trajectory of life, when asked by an agnostic if he supposed "mankind grew better or grew worse or remained the same," Chesterton answered that "it might depend on how mankind chose to go on."[27] In other words, the future state of humanity is contingent upon current decisions, which are indeed

26. Chesterton, 137.
27. Chesterton, *Everlasting Man*, 408.

effective in changing the future course. In the same passage, he suggests that life is not an unwavering line or curve, as if it were to reach a particular point on a graph without redirection.[28] Just because one may head in every direction before arriving at the final point does not dismiss the possibility of fate, except Chesterton explicitly states that one makes willful decisions according to his liking, "going where he like[s] and stopping where he cho[oses], going into a church or falling down in a ditch."[29]

That the story could end in any way is consistent with the Catholic conception of heaven and hell, either of which we have a part in choosing by the actions of this life. Chesterton suggests that the moral life is thrilling in that every "instant" is "an immortal crisis" since each moral choice is a matter of life and death.[30] "Will a man take this road or that?—that is the only thing to think about, if you enjoy thinking," suggests Chesterton. The moment of death is one that Chesterton calls "exciting" and suggests is a strong instance of free will: "You can finish a story how you like." If not at the moment of death, then by all of life's free actions one will have given an answer.[31]

This is not to suggest a Pelagian view in which one merits heaven or hell in direct proportion to the quality of one's actions. Salvation is ultimately for God to give, but the economy of salvation is such that God allows mankind to freely accept and participate in the salvation he offers. For these reasons, Chesterton denies elements of fate even within the Christian tradition, an example of which is Calvinist predestination. Chesterton considers predestinarian beliefs to rob life of its excitement because they ultimately are a denial of the great gift of free will:

---

28. Chesterton, 408.
29. Chesterton, 408.
30. Chesterton, *Orthodoxy*, 138.
31. Chesterton, 138.

To the Catholic every other daily act is dramatic dedication to the service of good or of evil. To the Calvinist no act can have that sort of solemnity, because the person doing it has been dedicated from eternity, and is merely filling up his time until the crack of doom. . . . The difference is that to a Christian of my kind this short earthly life is intensely thrilling and precious; to a Calvinist like Mr. Shaw it is confessedly automatic and uninteresting. To me these threescore years and ten are the battle. To the Fabian Calvinist (by his own confession) they are only a long procession of the victors in laurels and the vanquished in chains. To me earthly life is the drama; to him it is the epilogue.[32]

As it relates to story, predestination casts life as the resolution of the story, not a story as it plays out in the decisions of the characters. Life must end a certain way, so freedom is an illusion, and the instant loses its dramatic features as a moral decision goes from affecting eternity to affecting only aspects of earthly life without relevance to eternity. We might suppose that God is taking us seriously when he lets our actions mean what they do, answering for how we wish to live in this life and the next life. For Chesterton, this spiritual truth allows him to compare life to a "serial story" in which "life ends with the promise (or menace) 'to be continued in our next.'"[33] For the second installment of a story series to ignore the actions of its characters in the first would be a poor serial story.

While Chesterton asserts that a story may end in any way, this does not mean that he believes it ought to end in any way, as if one ending were just as good as another. Every author, by virtue of the willful choice of every detail, has an ultimate purpose for the characters. An author sets a standard for how the

32. G.K. Chesterton, *What's Wrong with the World*, in *The Collected Works of G.K. Chesterton* (San Francisco: Ignatius, 1987), 4:153–154.

33. Chesterton, *Orthodoxy*, 138.

story ought to end, but the characters have the freedom to make decisions that will bring them closer to or further from achieving this purpose. This metaphor begins to shed some light on the relationship between the free will of the author and that of the characters in the story. The romance that arises from this principle, as well as the other aforementioned principles of a story, lends to the drama of life, which we will next consider.

CHAPTER 2

The Genre of Romance

"But nearly all people I have ever met in this western society in which I live would agree to the general proposition that we need this life of practical romance; the combination of something that is strange with something that is secure. We need so to view the world as to combine an idea of wonder and an idea of welcome. We need to be happy in this wonderland without once being merely comfortable."[1]

INFLUENCES ON CHESTERTON'S ROMANTICISM

While many different types of stories are important to Chesterton and are often representative for him of human life, such as detective stories and fairytales, the type of story that perfuses his works and seems to pop up explicitly every few lines is the romance story. Romance is part and parcel of Chesterton's worldview of life as a story. In fact, from a consideration of the ideals of romance compared to other genres through Chesterton's perspective, we can ultimately arrive at the conclusion that romance is the ideal genre that the story of life ought to take on. The moral imperative for the story to be a romance story will become more evident when considering what romance represented for Chesterton—namely, a fight for the achievement of good, an exhilarating love that drives the protagonist to seek the good of the one who is loved, the thrift of freedom within a world of

---

1. G.K. Chesterton, *Orthodoxy* (Park Ridge, IL: Word on Fire Classics, 2017), 3.

limits, and the adventure of life arising from the real dangers and drastic consequences of human decisions.

Lest Chesterton's ideal of romance be dismissed as a bias derived from early life experiences or the sentimental longings of a hopeless romantic or an ideal simply adopted from the British and American Romanticism literary movements that Chesterton admired in part, the ideal of romance is much bigger and beyond the personal tastes of Chesterton. In fact, it is a set of principles that have been represented and defended by the Christian tradition up and down the centuries. It would not be inaccurate or reductive to say that the Christian story of salvation is the quintessential romance story. Far more ancient than any romantic musings of Percy Bysshe Shelley or Walt Whitman, the Christian story tells the narrative of a cosmic battle of good and evil, wherein humanity's entire earthly existence is a struggle against the onslaught of evil, which only a divine being could save them from out of love for the people he created. This cosmic narrative of salvation history was of ultimate significance for Chesterton, and how the principles of romance are expressed by this cosmic story will be explored further. For now, let us first consider the core influences on Chesterton's romanticism before assessing the key principles of romance from Chesterton's perspective.

Chesterton's Toy Theater

Where did Chesterton's romantic worldview begin? We can trace it back to his childhood home in the Kensington area of London. It was during these humble beginnings in the 1870s that the young Chesterton would first encounter the toy theater, a play device that he would continue to use for the rest of his life even into adulthood. Long before the grown G.K. Chesterton would cut out and color the cardboard characters for his self-written and self-directed plays, it was his creative father who ran the show for his two young sons, Gilbert and his brother, Cecil: "He [Mr. Edward Chesterton] wrote the plays. He drew, cut out and pasted up the actors and actresses (which were only a few inches high), and he acted as stage-director, carpenter and scene-shifter."[2] It is remarkable to consider that all of G.K. Chesterton's works, his creative mind, and his romantic worldview were largely influenced by a simple, imaginative, and homemade toy theater set.

Deep into his married life, Chesterton would continue this playful practice that he learned from his father. In their house in Battersea soon after his marriage to Frances Blogg, Chesterton would write plays for his toy theater and cut out and color cardboard characters and scenery,[3] not only putting on plays for his own pleasure but also entertaining the neighborhood children.[4] When later settling down to live in Beaconsfield, there, too, Chesterton would put on his plays for the local children. Fr. John O'Connor, the inspiration for Chesterton's character Fr. Brown, remarked about the figure behind the local spectacle, "He is incurably romantic. For his own amusement—and the real enjoyment it invariably gives to about two hundred neighborhood children—he has constructed a toy theatre in which the most incredible melodramas and farces are produced with the greatest gusto."[5]

The toy theater was far more than a mere pastime for Chesterton. For one, the toy theater was characteristic of play, in both senses of the word. All throughout his life, Chesterton would consider children's play to be a more serious act than any of the writing he would ever do, a claim as serious as it may be

2. Joseph Sheridan, "The Boyhood of G.K. Chesterton," in *The Catholic Boy*, May 1957, article, box 2 in G.K. Chesterton Collection, University of Notre Dame Rare Books & Special Collections, Notre Dame, IN (hereafter cited as GKC Collection), 18–19.

3. G.K. Chesterton, "The Toy Theatre," leaflet, no. 200 in Printed Ephemera I, GKC Library. Also published as "The Toy Theatre" in *Tremendous Trifles*.

4. George Knollys, "Mr. Gilbert Keith and His Toy Theatre," GKC Library, 617.

5. John O'Connor, "Gilbert Keith Chesterton," *PAX* 12, no. 4 (January 1936): 108, box 2, GKC Collection.

self-deprecating.[6] Furthermore, a simple play (in the sense of a drama) was a powerful vehicle capable of expressing the deepest philosophy. Just as the Greek tragedies evoked the full range of human emotions and questions about meaning and morality, Chesterton claimed the same revelatory power about the plays of his toy theater: "My toy theatre is as philosophical as the drama of Athens."[7] The toy theater expressed the "the main principle of art"—namely, that art "consists of limitation," from the frame of the toy theater to the trimming of cardboard characters.[8] Even within the small bounds of the frame, there existed such creative potential for writing plays and making characters that told a much larger story and symbolized a much more profound reality. As Chesterton put it, "By reducing the scale of events it can introduce much larger events. . . . Because it is small it could easily represent the Day of Judgment. . . . You can only represent very big ideas in very small spaces."[9]

The plays of Chesterton's toy theater were able to represent a much larger story through the power of symbolism, which is, in a sense, a form of limitation. The cosmic realities of good and evil, for example, could be represented by the colors white and black in the tiny cardboard figures. Chesterton considered the significance of his plays to lie largely in the symbols, colors, and minute details of his characters, claiming that "indeed the whole art of making a play for the toy theatre consists in making as much as possible of it depend on these emblems and external signs."[10] One elucidatory example lies in his play *St. George and the Dragon*, which he wrote for his toy theater while living in

6. Chesterton, "The Toy Theatre."
7. Chesterton, "The Toy Theatre."
8. Chesterton, "The Toy Theatre."
9. Chesterton, "The Toy Theatre."
10. Chesterton, "The Toy Theatre."

YOUR LIFE IS A STORY

Battersea.[11] Chesterton accentuated certain symbolic details in the characters of this play, such as the bright red-and-white shield and the halo of St. George, as well as the fierce dragon (see fig. 1 & 2).[12] The purpose of the details was to powerfully allude to the greater cosmic reality behind the story. The audience would find the frame of the theater, containing the tiny characters of the play, to be a window into a deeper reality. When they noticed that the character St. George had the tumultuous decision "of becoming a saint or to remain uncanonised," they might have remembered their own moral choices between heroism and mediocrity in real life.[13] Chesterton achieved this dramatic effect by making multiple versions of the character St. George, one with a halo and another without. All things considered, the toy theater proved to be both a key influence on and representation of Chesterton's romantic worldview, planting the earliest seeds of a view of limits, play, and romance that would undergird his view of life as a story from then on.

11. Knollys, "Mr. Gilbert Keith and His Toy Theatre," 617. Many of the characters and scenery pieces from this play are still extant at the Notre Dame London Global Gateway archive (GKC Library). Additionally, a full outline of the play *St. George and the Dragon* is etched in one of Chesterton's notebooks, currently at the British Library (Reference: Add MS 73355 D [c 1907]).

12. Chesterton, "The Toy Theatre."

13. Knollys, "Mr. Gilbert Keith and His Toy Theatre," 619.

Figure 1. Photograph of the blue dragon and blue devils from the toy theater collection. G.K. Chesterton Library, University of Notre Dame London Global Gateway, London, UK.[14]

Figure 2. Photograph of the blue dragon, St. George, and princess characters from the toy theater collection. G.K. Chesterton Library, University of Notre Dame London Global Gateway, London, UK.

14. In an early tale titled "Half Hours in Hades: An Elementary Handbook of Demonology" (1891), the young Chesterton identifies the blue devil as the devil of pessimism, which most frequently makes its home among the noble class. Interestingly, Chesterton depicts the dragon and devils as blue in his toy theater set.

American and British Romanticism

In addition to the early influence of the toy theater, another significant influence on Chesterton's romantic worldview was the American and British Romanticism literary movements. While Chesterton may not have been a full proponent of all the figures of this movement on either side of the Atlantic, a figure that Chesterton praises and traces his worldview to is Walt Whitman. An author who expressed great wonder at creation, Whitman epitomized for Chesterton the "joie de vivre," which helped carry Chesterton from his nihilistic art-school years toward a life of gratitude and wonder lived in the Catholic Church. Having "hung on to the remains of religion by one thin thread of thanks," Chesterton attributes this major turning point in his life to the writings of Walt Whitman, Robert Browning, and Robert Louis Stevenson. The elements of this romantic movement contribute greatly to Chesterton's worldview of gratitude to God for existence and for the small, often overlooked things that are indeed created with design and intention.

Influenced by both the toy theater that his father introduced to him at a young age and the Romanticism literary movements, Chesterton's romantic worldview saturates every page of his writing, from a delicious description of the world around him to the most solemn philosophical claims. If life was a story for Chesterton, then romance was the dramatic shape and defining trajectory of the quintessential human story. Romance encompassed and best expressed Chesterton's deepest intuitions about life—namely, that life has inherent limits, that life is thrilling because of (not in spite of) its limits, and that there exists a strong sense of the "good" (in both abstract and concrete forms) that ought to be defended. Far more than an intuition, these characteristics of romance are in fact strong philosophical claims about human freedom and purpose. In particular, romance claims that human freedom must operate within the bounds of inherent limits, however paradoxical it is to say that freedom is inherently limited.

Likewise, it proposes that human purpose arises from a sort of battle, such that it would be hard to imagine a meaningful story that did not involve a struggle and an overcoming of conflict. In summary, Chesterton's far-reaching romantic worldview can be understood under the following characteristics, each of which grants depth, shape, and purpose to the human story: adventure, fighting and loving, chivalry, and thrift.

ROMANCE: ADVENTURE

Treating the first characteristic, romance as an exciting adventure is very indicative of Chesterton's view of life and his defense of the Catholic Church, which he claims "went in specifically for dangerous ideas; she was a lion tamer."[15] Romance, which Chesterton suggested is a product of Christianity, conveys a sense of danger and excitement, "for romance consists in thinking a thing more delightful because it is dangerous; it is a Christian idea."[16] This notion of romance as dangerously thrilling is tied in with his view of life as a story, since the end of the story is largely dependent upon the actions and intentions of the faithful believer. Salvation is not guaranteed, and the Christian who summons the courage to accept this reality can rejoice at the responsibility to guard this one life—the only one given—from assaulting dangers that threaten the attainment of the good. Because of the elements of danger on our spiritual journeys, the adventure of life becomes "an opportunity" to avoid dangers and conquer evil in pursuit of the good.[17]

The romantic elements of thrift and fighting and loving are also present here. In the passage in which he speaks of the "thrilling romance of Orthodoxy," which is anything but "heavy, humdrum, and safe," he offers an illuminating image that expresses

15. Chesterton, *Orthodoxy*, 99.
16. G.K. Chesterton, *Heretics*, in *The Collected Works*, 1:126.
17. Chesterton, *Orthodoxy*, 50.

the improbability of being in the one right position: "It is always simple to fall; there are an infinity of angles at which one falls, only one at which one stands. . . . But to have avoided them all has been one whirling adventure."[18] While this may be more of a helpful image than a definitive claim about reality, Chesterton seems right to point out the objective scale of truth; all positions that one can assume are determined relative to the one right position, the objective standard.

Moreover, Chesterton mentions in the next chapter of *Orthodoxy* that he heard this statement, as if God were giving him an answer about the ideal trajectory of his life: "You will have real obligations, and therefore real adventures when you get to my Utopia. But the hardest obligation and the steepest adventure is to get there."[19] Here, Chesterton relates obligation to adventure as if to claim that having responsibility is what makes life exciting and eternal life worth striving for. To know ahead of time that our actions contribute nothing to our salvation would seem to rob the excitement from our moral actions, each of which has eternal consequences. Perhaps Chesterton hinted at a similar problem when he noticed the vibrancy of Christian morality being replaced by the dullness of social propriety: "The romance of conscience has been dried up into the science of ethics; which may well be called decency for decency's sake."[20]

At the same time, Chesterton guards against the notion of a thrilling adventure as something earned. Rather than being earned, the adventure must be given and must take one by surprise: "For with the removal of all question of merit or payment, the soul is suddenly released for incredible voyages. . . . A man cannot deserve adventures; he cannot earn dragons and hippogriffs. The mediaeval Europe which asserted humility gained

18. Chesterton, 100.
19. Chesterton, 123.
20. Chesterton, *What's Wrong with the World*, 112.

Romance; the civilization which gained Romance has gained the habitable globe."[21] Here, Chesterton is upholding medieval romanticism as an ideal to replicate, for the adventures of life, if they are to be most exciting, must be given by God and humbly received. He puts it another way pages later: "Adventures are to those to whom they are most unexpected—that is, most romantic. Adventures are to the shy: in this sense adventures are to the unadventurous."[22] The paradox of the beatitude "Blessed are the meek, for they will inherit the earth" (Matt. 5:5) is one that comes to mind as expressing this truth; in fact, Chesterton himself connects the two ideas.[23] Maybe it is not an accident but an expression of this paradoxical truth that God has tended to call the weak, the poor, or the least adventurous to a divinely appointed mission that would never leave them or the world the same. Indeed, we see in all of these cases that "adventure . . . is a thing that chooses us, not a thing that we choose."[24]

ROMANCE: FIGHTING AND LOVING

Second, the notion of fighting and loving is a key expression of Chesterton's romanticism, one that perfuses his defense of patriotism and perhaps is best expressed by the story of St. George. The story of St. George was beloved by Chesterton, one that seemed to have personal significance for him for many reasons. In a well-known passage characteristic of Chestertonian paradox, he explains how the Church is able to uphold two extremes at once, "like the red and white upon the shield of St. George. It has always had a healthy hatred of pink."[25] The national flag of England, bearing this red-and-white pattern of its patron saint, is a symbol that Chesterton draws upon to defend paradox and

21. Chesterton, *Heretics*, 71–72.
22. Chesterton, 74.
23. Chesterton, 69.
24. Chesterton, 142–144.
25. Chesterton, *Orthodoxy*, 96.

patriotism, fighting for and loving one's nation. *St. George and the Dragon* was one of many plays that Chesterton wrote for his homemade toy theater. The character collection for this play contains many versions of the three main characters—St. George, the dragon, and the princess—to track the progression of a dramatic battle of which St. George proves to be the victor, though not without the cost and romanticism of fighting. Regarding these three characters very familiar to him, Chesterton offers a very clear and important parsing of romance:

> In every pure romance there are three living and moving characters. For the sake of argument they may be called St. George and the Dragon and the Princess. In every romance there must be the twin elements of loving and fighting. In every romance there must be the three characters: there must be the Princess, who is a thing to be loved; there must be the Dragon, who is a thing to be fought; and there must be St. George, who is a thing that both loves and fights.[26]

In this short passage, Chesterton establishes a framework for understanding romance, accounting for the two necessary elements of loving and fighting and the three categories into which persons or entities will fall. Of course, the Christian imagery is evident in the characters and the story of St. George. The story alludes strongly to the book of Revelation, which tells of the Lamb who defeats the devouring dragon and who is the Bridegroom of the heavenly Jerusalem (Rev. 20–21). The three main characters in the play have broad application to Christian truth, since this story is representative of Chesterton's romantic worldview, which has relevance to the entire Christian tradition. One

---

26. G.K. Chesterton, *Appreciation and Criticisms of the Works of Charles Dickens*, in *The Collected Works of G.K. Chesterton* (San Francisco: Ignatius, 1989), 15:255.

possible application is to view the devil as a personal adversary to one's own story, and one is fighting to guard his beloved soul from the powers of hell. Another is Chesterton's idea of patriotism: "That a thing must be loved *before* it is loveable."[27]

In fact, Chesterton's idea of "patriotism" is integral to his view of romance, and this notion of patriotically fighting for and defending the good goes hand in hand with his view of life as a story. What is the relationship between patriotism and story? Patriotism, as the alternative to optimism and pessimism, as Chesterton explains in "The Flag of the World," chapter 5 of *Orthodoxy*, is the proper approach to one's story. If one's story is not "loveable" in its current state—in the sense that one is not satisfied with his habits, decisions, and life trajectory—one must love it into becoming loveable. If it is on the right trajectory, one must actively keep it on the right trajectory, because there always exists the possibility that it goes off-kilter. One must love his story, because just as a "man belongs to this world before he begins to ask if it is nice to belong to it," one is given his life before he can question its details and trajectory.[28] As will be explored later on, the devil is the ultimate "anti-patriot," the enemy of our stories and the antithesis of the attitude we are meant to take toward life. Like the pessimist, we are meant to chastise, but unlike the pessimist, we must love what we are chastising. Like the optimist, we must be hopeful about what we are fighting for, but unlike the optimist, we must love it without reason and for its own sake rather than for some conception of it or for a particular aspect of it.

Though the application of fighting, loving, and patriotism to life may seem like an abstraction, for Chesterton, the romantic idea of fighting and loving is far from unrealistic. Romanticism is not the opposite of realism, just as he points out in *Heretics*

27. Chesterton, *Orthodoxy*, 45 (emphasis in original).
28. Chesterton, 64.

that serious is not the opposite of funny.[29] "It is idle," he says, "in speaking of war, to pit the realistic against the romantic, in the sense of the heroic; for all possible realism can only increase the heroism; and therefore, in the highest sense, increase the romance."[30] The romantic stories that fill the air, including "tales about gods and ghosts and the invisible king," are not mere fabrications unrelated to eternal truths; rather, these three types of tales can be said to point to their real Christian counterparts —gods point to God, ghosts point to the soul and spiritual realm, and the invisible king points to the divine sovereign over creation.[31] Just so, the ceaseless production of stories about battles and falling in love are clear "evidence of the eternal interest of the theme" of romance as well as the realism of the truths they convey.[32] For instance, fighting and loving can appear purely sentimental until the inevitable encounter with sacrifice and hardship, when love must transform from a feeling into a self-forgetting commitment that will not raise the white flag of surrender when the circumstances are dire. Perhaps the best exemplar for Chesterton of romanticism's realism is Christian marriage—"the chief subject and centre of all our romantic writing"—because the lovers' commitment to each other is proven to be authentic by virtue of promising the rest of their lives to each other and no other person. The "happily ever after" promise at the end of romantic tales is a hope that only fighting and loving can bring to fruition.

29. Chesterton, *Heretics*, 159–160.

30. G.K. Chesterton, *The Superstition of Divorce*, in *The Collected Works of G.K. Chesterton* (San Francisco: Ignatius, 1987), 4:274–275.

31. G.K. Chesterton, *The Everlasting Man*, in *The Everlasting Man: A Guide to G.K. Chesterton's Masterpiece*, ed. Dale Ahlquist (Elk Grove Village, IL: Word on Fire, 2023), 451.

32. Chesterton, 451.

ROMANCE: CHIVALRY

Chivalry, a medieval ideal important to Chesterton, could be considered a subcategory of the second expression of romance— that is, fighting and loving. Chesterton defines chivalry as "not the romantic, but the realistic, view of the sexes."[33] Chesterton is not pitting realism against romanticism, since authentic realism heightens romance. Rather, Chesterton is again objecting to the understanding of the romantic as the purely sentimental. He is right to do so in a modern culture that would dismiss chivalry as a medieval ideal that is no longer an ideal for a sophisticated secular society. For Chesterton, to defend chivalry as realistic is to suggest that this view of the sexes has truths that are relevant even in his time. In fact, he would even go so far as to suggest that chivalry is in practice far more real, fulfilling, and true to humanity than contractual marriage. A modern expression of chivalrously courting one woman is the lifelong act of "keeping to one woman" (in the sense of steadfast monogamy), which manifests the reality that the woman is worth fighting for and has the honor and power of deciding if the man is worthy of her.[34] Dropping the medieval details of castles, dragons, and suits of armor, this expression of faithfulness is real in that it is both still possible and very difficult. Yet somehow this chivalrous ideal of unworthiness opens one's eyes to see greater joys than if one were to think himself worthy of everything. Rather than complaining about being bound to his wife for the rest of his life, Chesterton marvels that he has the honor of "seeing one woman" at all.[35] To wish for other women would be to incapacitate the man from wonder at the opposite sex; to wish for all would be to lose them all.[36] Chesterton traces the losses of these chivalrous

---

33. G.K. Chesterton, *The Thing: Why I Am a Catholic*, in *The Collected Works of G.K. Chesterton* (San Francisco: Ignatius, 1990), 3:170.

34. Chesterton, *Orthodoxy*, 53.

35. Chesterton, 53.

36. Chesterton, 53–54.

ideals to pride: "Pride is a weakness in the character; it dries up laughter, it dries up wonder, it dries up chivalry and energy."[37]

Interestingly, Chesterton equates the Catholic treatment of Mary with chivalry,[38] in which her loyal sons and daughters love her and give her honor as the mother of their king. While romanticism might be perceived by some as viewing the world in a dreamy or gushy manner for its own sake, Christianity distinguishes the means from the end by suggesting that pleasing God and Mary is the goal, but doing so casts a "supernatural light on natural things," leading to greater joys than those resulting from seeking natural things for their own sake.[39] The story of Our Lady's Tumbler conveys these sentiments for Chesterton, as the tumbler stands on his head not to see the world differently but to please Mary, which in turn allows him to see the world differently but in a higher way.[40] From monogamy to Mary, Christianity can be considered to contain core romantic ideals that are practical in their application, difficult in their achievement, and fruitful in their accomplishment.

ROMANCE: THRIFT

Just as with the three other expressions of Chesterton's romanticism, understanding the romantic idea of thrift will be key in understanding the limits inherent to life. In his defense of thrift, Chesterton suggests that "economy is far more romantic than extravagance."[41] He reiterates this firm conviction in a telling book chapter called "The Romance of Thrift": "Thrift is the really romantic thing; economy is more romantic than

37. Chesterton, *Heretics*, 107.

38. G.K. Chesterton, *The Autobiography of G.K. Chesterton*, in *The Collected Works of G.K. Chesterton* (San Francisco: Ignatius, 1988), 16:85.

39. G.K. Chesterton, *St. Francis of Assisi*, in *The Collected Works*, 2:70.

40. Chesterton, 70.

41. Chesterton, *Orthodoxy*, 60.

extravagance. . . . Thrift is poetic because it is creative."[42] Thrift is creative in the sense of ordering the limited materials of this life to create something more meaningful than the sum of its parts. This characterization of thrift as creative is essential to an understanding of human free will as a creative capacity to order the materials of this life to become more meaningful—that is, more aligned to reality, more like life, and in stronger connection to objective values.

While different philosophical camps may quarrel about the extent to which human freedom is limited, Chesterton no doubt perceives thrift and limits as inherent to this life and to human freedom. Each person has only one life to live, and every moment of every day is unrepeatable. No two decisions are ever the same, because time will have passed, and the circumstances of the decision will be different even if the object of the decision is the same. Rather than trying to deny this reality or theorize away the weight of each moment, the Christian perceives the divine economy at work through thrift and limits, and the acknowledgment of one's responsibility in each moment can give rise to the thrilling view of the moral life that views every moral decision as bearing upon eternity and presenting an opportunity to achieve the good.

Why else is thrift romantic? Thrift, as already seen in the moral life, grants greater value to the few things that one has to make good use of, including this one life, one's possessions, and life's circumstances. The novel *Robinson Crusoe*, which tells of a man who must survive a shipwreck using an eclectic assortment of salvaged items, is an allegory for Chesterton of human existence. Chesterton explains how one could view in a practical way the contingency of created things, even those things most mundane: "It is a good exercise, in empty or ugly hours of the

---

42. G.K. Chesterton, *What's Wrong with the World*, in *The Collected Works*, 4:120–121.

day, to look at anything, the coal-scuttle or the book-case, and think how happy one could be to have brought it out of the sinking ship on to the solitary island."[43] This way of seeing things, much more than a thought experiment, perceives the contingency of all things in a way that even a nonreligious person could understand. For instance, even if the unbeliever will not accept the classic Christian assumption about contingency that God is holding everything in existence, he could understand that the way things are presently could have been an infinitude of other ways. Even the unbeliever would grant that he only exists because of a particular sperm and egg of two particular people coming together, not to mention all the effects of the environment acting on him after conception. Whether one believes "that any man in the street is a Great Might-Not-Have-Been" can have drastic effects on one's treatment of others and one's own life.[44]

Moreover, thrift and limits take this life seriously and allow life to be exciting. In his autobiography, Chesterton expresses his love for bridges, which he describes as accentuating the bottomless abyss below; each step along the narrow swaying bridge is the difference between life and death.[45] It would not be a stretch to understand this image spiritually, with the gaping jaws of hell ready to consume the careless adventurer who falls off the bridge. This image alludes to Jesus' words about the narrow gate to heaven and the wide path to destruction (Matt. 7:13–14). Many other examples of thrift are evident throughout Chesterton's corpus, from the act of everyday decision-making to the sharing of marriage vows.

In sum, adventure, fighting and loving, chivalry, and thrift are the characteristics of Chesterton's conception of romance, and

---

43. Chesterton, *Orthodoxy*, 60.
44. Chesterton, 60.
45. Chesterton, *Autobiography*, 40.

far from being impractical, they are timeless ideals represented in the larger Christian tradition and granting form, depth, and meaning to our stories. As the ideal genre for the stories of our lives, romance establishes a framework through which to understand our role in the story, what makes life meaningful, and what are the bounds of meaning. Viewing life as a romance presents life as a dangerous tension between two primordial forces—good and evil—with the whole trajectory revolving around the central question "Which side will you choose?" Every decision is one with temporal and eternal implications.

Not only are these romantic principles applicable to each person's life, but they are also the principles of the Christian tradition, quintessentially represented in the larger story of salvation history. Even a cursory skimming of the Bible will reveal that the Christian God is a God of limits, a God of the high adventure, and a God in love. For a God beyond the world to enter the world and be killed is an extreme and unnerving act of limitation. To say that God loves the human race is a disarmingly bold claim about romance. There is no parallel example of an uncreated being (more precisely, *ipsum esse subsistens*, being itself) loving created beings. Nevertheless, the Christian story of salvation history is the quintessential romance story, and we now consider the strange shape and trajectory of this macrocosmic story, the story that all of our stories ought to comprise.

CHAPTER 3

The Story of Salvation History

"The primary thing that [Jesus] was going to do was to die. He was going to do other things equally definite and objective; we might almost say equally external and material. . . . The whole story moves on wings with the speed and direction of a drama, ending in an act beyond words."[1]

THE COSMIC STORY

The ultimate story, epitomizing every principle of romance and itself being comprised of every human story, is the story of salvation history proclaimed by the Christian tradition up and down the centuries. This cosmic story seeks to explain everything from the source and shape of existence to how every human across space and time should navigate life, and it is the highest adventure, precisely because of its universal applicability, its high standard for human excellence and decision-making, and the weight it attributes to the consequences of human choices, which not only have rippling effects on the world but also simultaneously (and mysteriously) determine one's eternal state. This contrasts greatly with other philosophical positions, such as materialism or subjectivism, some of which seek only to explain the temporal and material impact of human choices, while others assert personal choices as quite literally "personal" and having little

---

1. G.K. Chesterton, *The Everlasting Man*, in *The Everlasting Man: A Guide to G.K. Chesterton's Masterpiece*, ed. Dale Ahlquist (Elk Grove Village, IL: Word on Fire, 2023), 339.

impact on other people. Christianity does not subscribe to those positions but instead claims that more actions than not have a direct or indirect impact on others; even inaction is an action with multi-faceted consequences.

Moreover, the story of salvation history is a story about "fighting and loving" at its core. "Salvation," in the literal sense of healing, suggests that a wounded and diseased condition must be actively fought against in order to be healed. Evil is the ultimate disease, so to speak, threatening to corrupt every moral action and to derail the story. The Christian story, in contrast with many other philosophical and religious worldviews, asserts that good is primary, while evil is derivative and parasitic. In other words, good and evil are not equal forces. That being said, the Christian tradition recognizes the corruptive power of evil. Proximate and ultimate good must be sought after and fought for against the ceaseless onslaught of evil.

Regarding thrift, limits are inherent to the story of salvation history, and limits are upheld as good. Interestingly, throughout the Christian tradition, the all-powerful and unlimitable God not only expects his people to seek the good within the bounds of limits but also paradoxically presents himself as a "God of limits." To take an initial example, the way that the all-powerful God came to earth was an extreme paradox—a powerless human baby born to an impoverished set of parents in a little-known corner of a pre-technological world.

This peculiar point about how the Author entered into his own story is the hermeneutical key for understanding the cosmic narrative and how every human story is meant to fit into it. God did not just have characters, but he himself wanted to take on a human story, too, with all of its adventures and struggles, its set limits as well as its many choices, in order to redeem it from within, in order to surprise and outdo humanity and to go where no god would go, modeling what the ideal human story would be.

As the saying goes, familiarity breeds contempt—and not only contempt but also apathy and blindness to the obvious. Chesterton witnessed firsthand that familiarity with the Christian story bred cultural apathy and blindness to the most paradoxical story that answered every deep question and should leave everyone stammering in an attempt to make sense of its cosmic significance. Naturally, having the keen ability to see everything from an unexpected angle and turning every position on its head, Chesterton had a peculiar yet powerful way of presenting the Christian story to an increasingly secular culture—the Christian story is a story brimming with paradoxes that shatter every expectation, and it is a story that has a supernatural ability to provide cathartic relief and satisfaction for every human longing. It is a challenge to every person, especially the cultural Christians who have known the story of Christianity their entire lives, as if to say, "The story is not what you think it is. To say the story is meaningful or significant is an extreme understatement. If you are not left stammering at this story, then you have missed the entire point."

As will be seen, Chesterton presents the story as following a particular cosmic trajectory, but each cosmic event along the trajectory is full of paradox. The story begins with the fall, the original source of conflict without which the later events would not make much sense. The fall asserts that good is primary, and it sets up the remainder of the cosmic story. Skipping over this initial conflict is one of the main reasons for missing the point of the story—how God came to earth and why. To put it differently, to skip over the source and reality of evil is akin to walking into a theater performance during the penultimate act.

Interestingly, Chesterton characterizes the state of humanity after the fall as "paganism," which he rightfully understood, in its essence, as a "search" for God. The Jewish people were not the only ones waiting in longing for redemption; the pagans with their many gods, Chesterton argued, were likewise in pursuit of satisfaction of their deepest longings. The climactic event occurring after many thousands of years of longing would be the definitive answer to the longing of every human—the coming of God. But the coming of God, precisely because of the way he came, shattered every expectation and took humanity by surprise, which is likely why many Jews missed the significance of the event that was before their eyes. Yet for those who noticed its significance and had a true encounter with God, whether pagan or Jew, they could not deny that this is what humanity had been looking for. The answer was for all people past, present, and future. On the cross, Jesus even anticipated and answered the despair of every atheist to come, for, as Chesterton described the irony, God himself seemed for a moment to be an atheist.[2] He outdid even the atheist in his doubt and despair when God cried out to God, "Why have you abandoned me?" From then on, no man, even unto the furthest limits of despair, could claim that God did not know his suffering, loneliness, and isolation. For God did.

Finally, the Resurrection was far more than a happy resolution that cultures could thereafter commemorate with Easter eggs. As Chesterton keenly noticed, the Resurrection took place in a garden, bringing life definitively to where death once entered the human experience. The defeat of death reversed humanity's deepest sadness and despairing acquiescence—that death has the final say, that all these good things perish and have an end, and that whatever meaning we create on this earth is contingent upon earthly existence, which itself is fleeting.

But if God's coming to earth two thousand years ago was the climax of the story and the ultimate answer to every human longing, why does it appear that evil often has its grip on humanity, that the world is going off course, and that people

2. G.K. Chesterton, *Orthodoxy* (Park Ridge, IL: Word on Fire Classics, 2017), 140.

are growing increasingly hopeless? The answer lies in yet another paradox that explains the state of humanity on this side of God's coming until the end of time—that the victory of good and the resolution of the original conflict with evil is "already but not yet" established. The end of time will mark the ultimate resolution, wherein God will be victorious and the story of salvation history will conclude with the ultimate defeat of evil. This resolution is certain and has already been secured in the Crucifixion and Resurrection of Christ. But in a way that we may not be able to fully comprehend, God has intended that each human story—until the end of time—be an opportunity for people to freely participate in and contribute to the cosmic story with their lives and choices. How each person's story ought to mirror the romance story of Christ and fit into the cosmic story is the purpose of the following chapter, but first let us consider the dramatic and unanticipated trajectory of the cosmic story—the story of salvation history.

THE FALL

In order to understand the cosmic romance story of salvation history, which every man and woman is called to partake in, we must start at the beginning. Just as the Bible begins with a creation account to present an ideal through which the rest of history may be viewed, we must begin with the primordial ideal state of humanity before the fall in order to fully understand where humanity is going. This deference to the past is an authentically Christian move; it is a wise move that Chesterton makes in giving voice to the past by honoring tradition, which he calls the "democracy of the dead."[3] In contrast to many of his contemporaries, who were quick to ignore what nearly every human of the past had intuited—namely, that something is wrong with humanity—Chesterton defended their intuition as sane and

3. Chesterton, 43.

right. Not only is the majority of humanity right about what they sense to be a "fall," but also to view all of history in terms of the fall has tremendous effects on how we view humanity's potential, the forces of good and evil, and meaning in this world. Chesterton's view of the fall is summarized well in this passage:

> The Fall is a view of life. It is not only the only enlightening, but the only encouraging view of life. It holds, as against the only real alternative philosophies, those of the Buddhist or the Pessimist or the Promethean, that we have misused a good world, and not merely been entrapped into a bad one. It refers evil back to the wrong use of the will, and thus declares that it can eventually be righted by the right use of the will. Every other creed except that one is some form of surrender to fate. A man who holds this view of life will find it giving light on a thousand things; on which mere evolutionary ethics have not a word to say.[4]

As hinted in this passage, Chesterton's view of the fall has many important implications—the fall is a "view of life" through which all of history may be seen, "giving light on a thousand things"; the fall offers an "encouraging" perspective about humanity's potential and the world's primary goodness; the fall properly accounts for good and evil; and the fall defends free will and its proper use.

The Fall: A View of Life

As Chesterton rightly puts it, the fall is a "view of life" because it "giv[es] light on a thousand things."[5] This event of the long past is the lens through which to view where humanity has been, where humanity is now, and where humanity is heading.

4. G.K. Chesterton, *The Thing: Why I Am a Catholic*, in *The Collected Works of G.K. Chesterton* (San Francisco: Ignatius, 1990), 3:312.

5. Chesterton, 312.

If human history is a story, then the fall is the central conflict of the narrative of the human experience. The irony is that this primeval event, which has affected everything for the rest of history, cannot be known from direct experience; yet Chesterton notices that all of humanity strangely has a tangible experience of this central conflict from of old. The fall is not a modern theological intuition but a palpable experience of abnormality and lack that even history admits to: "The first is the fact that original sin is really original. Not merely in theology but in history it is a thing rooted in the origins. Whatever else men have believed, they have all believed that there is something the matter with mankind."[6] For Chesterton, the fall expresses the paradoxical truth that the normal is abnormal; even when life is going rightly, something is off: "The primary paradox of Christianity is that the ordinary condition of man is not his sane or sensible condition; that the normal itself is an abnormality."[7] The irony and the paradox is that the more normal and "natural" self is the self we have never known but the self we must become.[8]

The fall is a cheerful and encouraging perspective because it acknowledges the dignity of humanity, upholds the prelapsarian state of humanity as a tangible ideal to strive for, and accounts properly for good and evil. Though it is seemingly counterintuitive, Chesterton asserts in the words of his friend Fr. Waggett that "the doctrine of the Fall is the only cheerful view of human life."[9] Far from being a simple acquiescence that everything has gone wrong from the beginning, the fall is a grand statement of hope that at one point humanity was what it was meant to be and that it might one day recover this proper state. The fall presents the prelapsarian state as a "standard" of human

6. Chesterton, *Everlasting Man*, 71.

7. Chesterton, *Orthodoxy*, 161.

8. Chesterton, 161.

9. G.K. Chesterton, *The Autobiography of G.K. Chesterton*, in *The Collected Works of G.K. Chesterton* (San Francisco: Ignatius, 1988), 16:171.

flourishing without which progress is impossible. Chesterton criticizes his contemporary Robert Blatchford for seeking human progress without identifying the end goal to set the proper direction: "Without the doctrine of the Fall all idea of progress is unmeaning. Mr. Blatchford says that there was not a Fall but a gradual rise. But the very word 'rise' implies that you know toward what you are rising. Unless there is a standard you cannot tell whether you are rising or falling."[10] The final destination to which every human is called is already set as the objectively best outcome—humanity is meant to progress toward union with God, the effect of which is ontological fulfillment in joy and "beatitude." The fall acknowledges beatitude to be the ideal that humanity once possessed and has since lost.

The fall is also an assuring affirmation that we can know and sense our progress toward union with God and toward fulfillment of our purpose in his grand story. To reference an example used by Chesterton, to tell a male friend "Be a man" has a strong moral force toward improvement and virtue because you and your friend both know that he is not living up to his potential.[11] Buried deep down in our hearts is a memory of our potential, and our hearts cease to rest until that promising memory is awakened to guide us along the journey of recovering what was lost. Furthering this analogy, every life is a romantic story of recovery; it is a story of adventure in returning home after having lost one's way; it is a story of thrift in the use of the salvaged materials of a shipwreck, like the novel *Robinson Crusoe*; it is a story of fighting what is evil and loving what is good. These romantic elements are set up by the fall, and without the context of the original conflict, it would be hard to comprehend any sense of moral progress or character development in each person's life, much less in the cosmic story of salvation history.

10. G.K. Chesterton, *The Blatchford Controversies*, in *The Collected Works*, 1:385.
11. Chesterton, 385.

Finally, by setting up the prelapsarian state as a high standard for humanity, the fall acknowledges the tremendous dignity that humanity was given before the fall, part of which they retain after. Chesterton plays with the core Christian tenet of human dignity expressed in Genesis, which presents man and woman as created in God's image and likeness. He offers the image of a wooden statue in a garden as a representation for humanity. Before the fall, the statue served as a sort of "god of the garden" in which "the wood was graven or stamped with an image, deliberately, and from the outside; in this case the image of God."[12] All the plants and animals in the garden reverenced the statue as privileged to be in the image and likeness of the Creator. However, as a result of the fall, the statue fell and shattered into faintly reminiscent pieces of the original statue: "The statue has fallen from its pedestal and lies broken among the plants and weeds."[13] Taking together the high dignity and the tragic fall, humanity is "now both better and worse than the mere plants in the garden, which are perfect according to their own plan."[14] Humans are better than plants and animals since they have been created to be like God himself, but they are worse because they have lost, at least partially, the dignity they once had. All of human experience from this point has been marked by the tragic realization that humans lie in shattered pieces of their former glory. But even in this tragedy lies the hope that the divine architect might rebuild the statue so as to restore its former glory.

PAGANISM

If humanity's separation from God is the central conflict that every generation has experienced, all of humanity after this primordial conflict has been awaiting a resolution to this conflict.

12. Chesterton, *The Thing*, 311.
13. Chesterton, 311.
14. Chesterton, 311.

Whether or not generations would think of their pitiful state in these terms, ultimately they have felt that the good had been lost and that it needed to be recovered. This is how Chesterton defines the human race after the fall and before the coming of Christ—humanity was searching, but it never found the ultimate good it was searching for until Christ.[15]

While the fall may seem like an exclusively Christian belief, Chesterton argues that even the pagans were strongly marked by this sentiment. The pagans were not atheists; the pagans had "about half a dozen" religions, and although their many gods were not a perfect memory of the good that was lost, they expressed the search for the divine ordering of the world.[16] The pagans had a lost memory of glory, which is deeply rooted in their mythology and writings: "These men were conscious of the Fall, if they were conscious of nothing else; and the same is true of all heathen humanity. Those who have fallen may remember the fall, even when they forget the height. Some such tantalising blank or break in memory is at the back of all pagan sentiment."[17] The sentiment of recovery and search fills their poetry: "On that sublime sense of loss that is in the very sound of all great poetry, and nowhere more than in the poetry of pagans and sceptics. . . . Happiness is not only a hope, but also in some strange manner a memory; and that we are all kings in exile."[18]

Although Chesterton praises the pagans for their good qualities—such as civic obedience, reverence toward the divine through sacrifice, and the search for meaning and truth by means of mythology and philosophy—he names many problems that end in despair, an almost inevitable result without Christ, for whom they had ultimately been looking.[19] The first

15. Chesterton, *Everlasting Man*, 173.
16. Chesterton, *Heretics*, in *The Collected Works*, 1:122.
17. Chesterton, *Everlasting Man*, 138.
18. Chesterton, *The Thing*, 312.
19. Chesterton, *Heretics*, 122; Chesterton, *Everlasting Man*, 170, 412.

problem—eroticism and unnatural desires—arose from the fact that "pagans could only mix beauty with mortality."[20] In other words, without an ultimate explanation for death and the afterlife, paganism had to make good use of beauty during its fleeting moments on earth. But treating earthly beauty as ultimately satisfying led to one of two pitfalls. The pagan would either be too optimistic, claiming, "All natural things are good. War is as healthy as the flowers. Lust is as clean as the stars," or too pessimistic, acquiescing, "The flowers are at war. The stars are unclean. Nothing but man's conscience is right, and that is utterly defeated."[21]

Paganism was on the road to becoming unnatural because it was natural religion, not revealed religion: "The only objection to Natural Religion is that somehow it always becomes unnatural."[22] Though it was not wicked for paganism to find the pleasures and beauty of this life good, treating them as ultimate almost necessarily led to "natural passions becoming unnatural passions."[23] On this point, Chesterton makes a bold claim about the ultimate state of mythology: "I do not believe that mythology must begin with eroticism. But I do believe that mythology must end in it."[24] Without an ultimate explanation for beauty and passions, the deities and mythological creatures serve proxy for ultimate explanations, though their inadequacy as ultimate explanations is evident. What results from insufficient explanation is "staleness," which arises at the inevitable point "when the man is tired at playing at mythology and pretending that a tree is a maiden or that the moon made love to a man."[25] Existentially rebelling against these explanations, pagans "[sought] stranger

20. Chesterton, *Autobiography*, 270.
21. Chesterton, *Blatchford*, 384–385.
22. Chesterton, *Orthodoxy*, 74.
23. G.K. Chesterton, *St. Francis of Assisi*, in *The Collected Works*, 2:39–40.
24. Chesterton, *Everlasting Man*, 255.
25. Chesterton, 255.

sins ... as stimulants to their jaded sense."[26] The pagan world needed an ultimate explanation to renew the natural world. The answer awaited them east of the Mediterranean at a certain point in time—namely, the Incarnation of "the Christian God. He made Nature but He was Man."[27]

A related problem of paganism is that it was a search for its own sake. According to Chesterton, "Mythology is a *search*; it is something that combines a recurrent desire with a recurrent doubt."[28] Even if it did not begin as a search for its own sake, it became one, since paganism could never find the ultimate good it was searching for; it would ceaselessly express this desire for the good while always expressing doubt that it found the ultimate good. With a faint memory of the ideal good in mind but an inability to achieve it, the pagan would cry out until the coming of Christ, "Why cannot these things be?"[29] It would not be until Christianity that there would arise "a view of the universe satisfying all sides of life; a complete and complex truth with something to say about everything."[30] This would finally satisfy the "imaginative side" of the pagan and end his search in existential satisfaction.[31]

As a result of its devolving passions and unsatisfied search, paganism was marked by despair and sadness without an ultimate explanation to set right the natural and supernatural orders. Chesterton sums up the point here in suggesting that paganism was only happy in the passing pleasures of earth but was full of despair when ultimate explanations were required:

26. Chesterton, 291.
27. Chesterton, *Blatchford*, 384–385.
28. Chesterton, *Everlasting Man*, 174 (emphasis in original).
29. Chesterton, 177.
30. Chesterton, 193.
31. Chesterton, 193.

But it is all a gaiety about the facts of life, not about its origin. To the pagan the small things are as sweet as the small brooks breaking out of the mountain; but the broad things are as bitter as the sea. When the pagan looks at the very core of the cosmos he is struck cold. Behind the gods, who are merely despotic, sit the fates, who are deadly. Nay, the fates are worse than deadly; they are dead.[32]

The pagans were "struck cold" when realizing that all the natural pleasures, however good in themselves, were quickly passing away. Though only having a faint memory of the one true God, "that Unknown God [had] faded into a Fate" who would sever the strings of life at the end of this short existence.[33] As Chesterton wittingly puts it, paganism would be marked by "the presence of the absence of God" until Christ came.[34] Until that ultimate resolution of the central conflict of the fall, which pagan humanity experienced at its core, the search for and memory of God would serve as a placeholder until the returning presence of God.

THE STORY OF CHRIST

As epitomized in the pagans, postlapsarian humanity was searching for a resolution to the greatest conflict of separation from God. Chesterton claims that two needs would have to be met— the dual need for a meaningful story and for a truthful, logical explanation. On the one hand, pagan mythology was desirous of a story—an imaginative, dramatic expression of history that paid tribute to the beauty of the natural world. On the other hand, pagan philosophy demanded a true explanation for the current afflicted state of humanity. In short, mythology sought

32. Chesterton, *Orthodoxy*, 162.
33. Chesterton, *Everlasting Man*, 137.
34. Chesterton, 136–137.

meaning romantically expressed, and philosophy sought truth rationally conveyed. In Chesterton's opinion, nothing up to that point in history had been able to satisfy both sides of the pagan search. Right when the search seemed to have been abandoned in despair, a very strange event occurred that ended the search in satisfaction and addressed this double need—the long-lost God came to earth as a human being.

As Chesterton argues, Christ was the fitting answer to paganism's questions and the two-fold search. When the mythologist cried out about his ideals, "Why cannot these things be?"[35] the Incarnation of Christ proclaimed that these ideals are possible for him who was both a historical and ideal figure.[36] To the two-fold search of paganism, Christ presented himself as the protagonist of humanity's story: "It met the mythological search for romance by being a story and the philosophical search for truth by being a true story."[37] As Chesterton suggests here, it is vital that Christ—the ultimate reconciliation of the historical and the ideal, of the human and the divine, of the material and the spiritual, of the rational and the mystical, of the objective and the subjective—entered into the story and proved to be the true resolution to the conflict of separation from God.

Chesterton goes so far as to propose that such a climax of the grand story of humanity was most fittingly expressed as it was in the romantic, thrilling manner of God becoming man:

> The more deeply we think of the matter the more we shall conclude that, if there be indeed a God, his creation could hardly have reached any other culmination than this granting of a real romance to the world. Otherwise the two sides of the human mind could never have touched at all. . . . It was that

35. Chesterton, 177.
36. Chesterton, 412.
37. Chesterton, 412.

abyss that nothing but an incarnation could cover; a divine embodiment of our dreams.[38]

Though this argument is central to *The Everlasting Man*, decades earlier in his debates against Mr. Blatchford, Chesterton recognizes the repetition of the idea of a god becoming man in many religions and cultures as support for the Incarnation of Christ. He argues, "If we are so made that a Son of God must deliver us, is it odd that Patagonians should dream of a Son of God?" Continuing the argument, he claims, "It is tolerably plain, surely, that these two stories are common because the situation is an intensely probable and human one, because our nature is so built as to make them almost inevitable. Why should it not be that our nature is so built as to make certain spiritual events inevitable?"[39] Pagan mythology and philosophy had demanded a thrilling story that was true, and Christ satisfied these desires in a way the world never would have expected.

Like the larger narrative of salvation history starting with the fall, the life of Christ takes the form of a romance story, with its elements of surprise, thrift, paradox, adventure, and fighting and loving. Chesterton thinks it an understatement to call the life of Jesus Christ "the strangest story in the world."[40] It is a story full of paradoxes that convey the truths of existence in the most unexpected ways. First among the many startling events of Christ's life is his birth in Bethlehem, which Chesterton calls "a place where extremes meet," the definition of a paradox.[41] It was in a dark cave of Bethlehem that "omnipotence and impotence" and "divinity and infancy" were paradoxically coupled in a way never imagined.[42] It was here in a cave as a baby that God was to

38. Chesterton, 412.
39. Chesterton, *Blatchford*, 374–375.
40. Chesterton, *Everlasting Man*, 455.
41. Chesterton, 274.
42. Chesterton, 273.

begin reclaiming his rule over the world. Even Christ's Crucifixion was an event of many paradoxes. Somehow life itself experienced death, and somehow "God had been forsaken of God."[43] God went deeper into the despair of the human experience than we would have expected, to the point that even an atheist could find himself outmatched by God, who himself "seemed for an instant to be an atheist."[44]

The Birth of Christ

The birth of Christ, or what Chesterton calls "the miracle play of Bethlehem," was the first of many paradoxical events in the life of Christ, which, even if they could not have been anticipated, nevertheless satisfied the two-fold search of humanity up to God's fleshly arrival.[45] During this "first act of the divine drama," Christ had appeared not with the full power of heaven but as a baby "on a dark and curtained stage sunken out of sight."[46] Although it was a surprise, the surprise was gentle, as if it were a quiet yet very convincing reminder of who one was and what the world was about: "It is rather something that surprises us from behind, from the hidden and personal part of our being. . . . It is rather as if a man had found an inner room in the very heart of his own house, which he had never suspected; and seen a light from within."[47] The Incarnation of God had satisfied the need for anthropomorphism that pagan mythology had expressed, but the fulfillment of this desire was not without surprise. Paganism had many gods and goddesses of earth and sky, expressing an innate desire to relate to the forces of nature in the likeness of man. What was not expected was that God would deign to actually *make* himself a man to satisfy the deep longing of relating to

43. Chesterton, 348.
44. Chesterton, *Orthodoxy*, 140.
45. Chesterton, *Everlasting Man*, 291.
46. Chesterton, 276–277.
47. Chesterton, 294.

God. Chesterton describes the Incarnation as material for "a sensational novel . . . in which a number of separate characters all turned out to be the same character."[48] The entire natural world, formerly expressed anthropomorphically in pagan mythology, at last found its expression and fulfillment in the one who created all and made himself known as a baby: "And when the whole universe looks like a man we fall on our faces."[49] The surprise of the Incarnation was "much too good to be true, except that it [was] true."[50]

The Crucifixion

As important a moment as the birth of Christ was, the birth was only the opening act of the drama of Christ's life. It is equally morbid and ironic to state that the purpose of Christ's birth was to set him up for his death. In this strangest story of the world, the God, Jesus Christ, took on a human body so that it could experience death. Death was his sure objective; his life from the beginning was pointing toward a death that would once-and-for-all defeat the death that had always haunted and will continue to haunt humanity. Chesterton expresses the story of Christ in terms of a drama carried forth with mission and purpose toward the sacrifice that would restore life to humanity: "We are meant to feel that his life was in that sense a sort of love-affair with death, a romance of the pursuit of the ultimate sacrifice. . . . The whole story moves on wings with the speed and direction of a drama, ending in an act beyond words."[51] It may seem tragic and unbecoming to describe God as loving death, but what becomes clear from this language is that God loved the human race so much that he would rush to and embrace death so that humanity might be reunited to him again. Christ knew his mission from

48. Chesterton, 131.
49. G.K. Chesterton, *Heretics*, 120–121.
50. Chesterton, *Everlasting Man*, 272.
51. Chesterton, 339.

the beginning; God the Father called him to die, and he ran forth in obedience. We might understand this to be Christ's story, which fulfilled the pagan longing: "This is where it was a fulfilment of the myths rather than of the philosophies; it is a journey with a goal and an object," which was "death."[52] Christ received a clear purpose from God the Father, and he obediently carried it out to its completion, setting a perfect model and revealing the Trinity so that humanity may know from whom to receive its purpose in life.

In the grand story of salvation history, the Crucifixion might be considered the climax through which the overarching conflict, the fall, is overcome. Interestingly, the Crucifixion itself answers the conflict of the fall with its own conflicts, in the paradoxical sense of extremes coming together. The very fact of the Crucifixion is a paradox in which the immortal God dies in his human nature. As Chesterton purports, to simply hear a story of a god dying for humanity would evoke a profound emotional response.[53] To hear about a "god sacrific[ing] himself to himself" ought to evoke "a thrill."[54] But far from being a simple sentimental story about a deity loving humanity to the point of death, the story itself is true. Christ's death was historical, and it has been rightfully considered by Christians as the most important and most efficacious event in all of history because it has tangible effects for all time. Every human person past, present, and future experiences the conflict of the fall, which allows evil to disturb one's story ordered toward union with God. But every human being can experience the salvific power of Christ's death, which definitively defeated evil and ensured that good will ultimately prevail. Though individual souls will show by the degree of obedience to their life stories whether they receive the effects of

52. Chesterton, 339.
53. Chesterton, *The Thing*, 237.
54. Chesterton, 302.

Christ's victory over evil, this climax of the cosmic story ensured that evil would not have the final say.

The Resurrection

In this grand story of salvation that began with the fall, the Resurrection is the recovery of humanity's story. The story of salvation began in a garden where humanity fell from grace. Chesterton picks up on this detail, noticing how "in a semblance of the gardener God walked again in the garden" on the day of Christ's Resurrection.[55] For Chesterton, the Resurrection marked "the first day of a new creation, with a new heaven and a new earth."[56] If in Christ's death and burial the search of pagan mythology and philosophy died and was buried, the Resurrection was assurance that the search was over because the God that man lost in the primordial garden had returned to be with mankind once again in a garden. The old order had passed away, and the search was over. We might even say that the story of humanity had been resurrected.

What might seem like an inconsequential detail about Christ's resurrected body actually further supports this interpretation—Christ did not take on a different body from the one that experienced death. His resurrected body was a glorified body, but that body still bore the wounds of death. In fact, Christ's body would forever bear the five wounds that humanity caused in the original sin and in every sin thereafter. Christ chose not to erase the wounds that the supreme conflict of the fall caused.

If the Crucifixion is the act of sacrifice through which Christ overcame evil, the Resurrection is the assurance and manifestation of the victory of good over evil. Up to this point in time, death was the ultimate relativization of meaning. Pagan poetry, as Chesterton highlights, is an elucidating example of how

55. Chesterton, *Everlasting Man*, 349.
56. Chesterton, 349.

mankind viewed death as having the final say. The Resurrection is the promise that life after death is possible. Even if after the Resurrection evil appears to be surviving and thwarting good, the uncontested victory of good in the life to come is actively making itself present in the Mystical Body of Christ on earth, which is the Church.

Ever since the event of the Resurrection, Christians have been participating in the stage of the story characterized as "already but not yet." For two thousand years, Christians have been looking back to the climax of the story and forward to its final resolution. If the life, death, and Resurrection of the God-man were the goal of humanity's search and victory of good "already" achieved, the Second Coming of the God-man at the end of time will mark the full manifestation of God's victory, which has "not yet" shown itself in full. The promise of the story's "happily ever after" was already granted two millennia ago, and Christians joyfully await the full realization of the promise while actively embodying it by their holy lives.

THE ESCHATON
Christ: The Last Thing

Where this story ends is the eschaton, or the "last thing," the resolution of the grand story of creation and its revelation to all rational beings. The eschaton is Christ, who is the last thing. Christ's coming a second and final time will mark the end of time and the end of the story of creation. Christ, the protagonist of the cosmic story, will fully reveal every detail of his story, including God's own intentions for creation, mankind's participation or lack thereof in the story, and God's act of restoring mankind's story through Christ. In the eschaton, we will play the "dual purpose" of "the text and an audience" in both comprising God's story and witnessing the telling of the greatest drama of all time.[57] Though we can now only imagine what that story will be like, while on earth we can live in such a way that we may participate in this story actively playing out, capacitating ourselves to joyfully receive this best of stories. When the book cover closes at the end of time, we will find ourselves integrated into Christ and his story either fully or not at all.

Heaven

In treating the end times specifically as the revelation of the conclusion of the grand story of creation, we might understand heaven as one's full incorporation into this story and joyful reception of it. Every major event of this grand story of salvation—the fall, Israel's covenant with God, the prophets, Christ's life, death, and Resurrection, the establishment of Christ's Church, the incorporation of the Gentiles—will find its full realization at the end of time. It will become completely clear, for instance, why God chose the people Israel out of the nations, why Christ came as a human at that point in history, and why Christ left humanity waiting for millennia for his Second Coming. Though Christians on earth cannot grasp the full implications of these events, the divine motivation will be revealed, and the souls who lived into these mysteries on earth with trust will find satisfaction in every detail of the story. It will be apparent how the great conflict of the fall was definitively resolved in the surprising events of Christ's life. All will perceive how the divine protagonist loved humanity to the point of becoming one of them and dying for them in a beautiful romance story of fighting, loving, and thrift. Christ the protagonist will have fully vanquished Satan, the cosmic anti-patriot and antagonist, who oppressed humanity and sought to destroy God's story. Those blessed souls in heaven will find themselves fully loved, fought for, won over, and reunited

57. Duncan Reyburn, *Seeing Things as They Are: G.K. Chesterton and the Drama of Meaning* (Eugene, OR: Cascade Books, 2016), 87.

with the God they had tragically lost. All of God's promises conveyed in the major and minor details of history will be proven true in the end.

A Complex Picture

Throughout his writings, Chesterton provides imagery to hint at what heaven and hell might be like. One perceptible theme is his view of heaven as a complex picture in which every soul is a unique color providing various hues and contrasts within the big picture. He alludes to this image here:

> If there is any certain progress it can only be [God's] kind of progress, the progress towards a complete city of virtues and dominations where righteousness and peace contrive to kiss each other. An impersonal force might be leading you to a wilderness of perfect flatness or a peak of perfect height. But only a personal God can possibly be leading you (if, indeed, you are being led) to a city with just streets and architectural proportions, a city in which each of you can contribute exactly the right amount of your own colour to the many coloured coat of Joseph.[58]

Chesterton intuits that heaven might be a complex work of art for many reasons. First, the trend toward complexity, especially a complexity of this kind in which millions of souls can find unity in this single reality, strongly suggests a personal force. God, in his divine intelligence, has made a final reality in which seemingly paradoxical virtues—like righteousness and peace, justice and mercy—might coexist. Second, comparing individuals to colors captures the uniqueness of each soul and the divine choice of how each soul might contribute to the big picture. We are reminded here of the point made earlier, that

58. Chesterton, *Orthodoxy*, 114.

"every colour has in it a bold quality as of choice."[59] It may very well be that God has a specific color for each individual to be during life and at the end of life. Sin could be considered as decreasing the intensity of our color. Throughout life we mix our colors with others' colors, perhaps becoming the desired color through the help of others. Third, Chesterton considers the complexity of heaven to be characteristic of Christianity, contrasted with other philosophies. As opposed to Buddhism, which idealizes the annihilation of self and the coalescing of all individuals into one being, Christianity idealizes the fullness of individuality within an objective unity. Chesterton grounds this claim in the Christian understanding that "God Himself is a society"[60] and that "love desires personality; therefore love desires division."[61]

Seeing the Whole

When all things are revealed, heaven will be the surreal experience of seeing the objective reality of existence and how one's life played a very small but nonetheless significant role in it. One will have the clear vision of how every action influenced oneself and others, rippling down the generations until the end of time. One would perceive how the lives of those existing long before him had contributed to his own small story and the grand story of creation.

This idea that one realizes his life is part of a colossal entity is one that Chesterton wished to write a book about. He claims about this "romance," one that he never had the chance to write, "Like every book I never wrote, it is by far the best book that I have ever written."[62] The romance story is about a young boy who travels away from his small farm and realizes upon looking back at his distant home and farm that they "were but parts of

59. Chesterton, 55.
60. Chesterton, 137.
61. Chesterton, 133.
62. Chesterton, *Everlasting Man*, 1.

some such gigantic figure, on which he had always lived, but which was too large and too close to be seen."[63] A Christian may immediately make the connection between the "gigantic figure" and the Body of Christ, a colossal reality wherein each Christian serves the role of a unique body part. Those souls who lived worthily and played their small roles in the grand story will be surprised beyond expectation when they find themselves part of the corporate whole they will one day see in its fullness.

Hell

The tragic alternative to being fully incorporated into God's story and celebrating every detail of the divine Author is to refuse participation in this story out of free will. While God's story is the epitome of unity as every moment of time, every detail of history, and every human being ever to live finds realization in this objective account, refusal of this unity is a legitimate option for rational beings with free will. Though God as Author and Protagonist will use every detail of the story to draw fallen mankind back to himself, individuals may wish to opt out of this narrative in order to create a narrative apart from God's. The problem with this obstinate mentality is that mankind, though possessing free will, does not have the same creative power as God to create another grand story equal to or greater than God's. If the eschaton is realizing how everyone and everything fits into the unity of God's storybook, hell might be perceived as an intentional ripping out of the page of one's life from the grand narrative in favor of a comparatively dull story. Standing alone, that one page would be a very short narrative that makes little sense on its own apart from the context of the original divine Author and other characters. Far from being the will of God that his characters rend themselves from his story, the absolute

63. Chesterton, 2.

separation between the author and the text is the result of separation initiated freely by man.

At the core of this decision is a free and prideful choice to prefer one's own illusion of a grand narrative to God's narrative. In the same passage where Chesterton presents individuals as arrows "feathered with free will" to hit the target of beatitude, he suggests the possibility that the arrows could redirect their course away from the target by the angling of their feathers.[64] Chesterton thinks that these souls would still bear the mark of this incredible gift of freedom in hell: "Since the freedom is itself a glory. In that sense they would still wear their haloes even in hell."[65] The arrows diverting their course would be making an intentional act to not hit the target.

Viewed another way, hell might be considered as the prideful choice to believe in oneself, as Chesterton alludes to in chapter 2 of *Orthodoxy*, "The Maniac." Commenting on the individualistic tendencies of his time, Chesterton imagines what the ultimate reality will be for someone who turned in on himself: "Then when the man, believing in nothing and in no man, is alone in his own nightmare, then the great individualistic motto shall be written over him in avenging irony . . . 'He believes in himself.'"[66] The prideful man believes in nothing apart from himself. He spends his life building up his own story at the expense of others, but the tragic outcome is that the only character in the story is himself. It is a rather one-sided and flat story compared to the grand story of creation, which involves millions of other characters, perspectives, and interwoven subplots. The prideful soul has lost the receptivity of welcoming the grand adventure given to him by the divine Author. Chesterton forebodes the anguish when one loses that state of receptivity:

64. Chesterton, *The Thing*, 150.
65. Chesterton, 150.
66. Chesterton, *Orthodoxy*, 20.

"The only simplicity that matters is the simplicity of the heart. If that be gone, it can be brought back by no turnips or cellular clothing; but only by tears and terror and the fires that are not quenched."[67] The soul that ripped its pages out of the grand story of creation will forever face that full realization that it rejected the best story for a pathetic narrative about oneself and only oneself. That same revelation of the grand story will be at once beatitude for the souls in heaven and anguish for the souls in hell.

67. Chesterton, *Heretics*, 112.

CHAPTER 4

The Trajectory of the Human Story

"Life (according to the faith) is very like a serial story in a maga-zine: life ends with the promise (or menace) 'to be continued in our next.'"[1]

MODELING THE HUMAN STORY
AFTER THE COSMIC STORY

As we have seen, not only is God the Author of the cosmic story of salvation history, but he also deigned to become a character in the story—not just a divine character but also a human character with a human story. The paradox that God took on a human story has major implications for the cosmic story, but we might now wonder what model God was intending to set for each human story. From an ontological perspective, we might wonder what objective standard and narrative archetype Jesus was estab-lishing by the example and trajectory of his own life. It would be too shallow to assume that Jesus' life, with its strange details and definitive divine actions, has little precedent to set for each human story. In fact, such an understanding would be inimical to the Christian tradition, which has consistently held that every person ought to become "another Christ" and to thereby discover

---

1. G.K. Chesterton, *Orthodoxy* (Park Ridge, IL: Word on Fire Classics, 2017), 138.

another dimension of meaning otherwise not achievable. Christ perfectly cooperated with the divine Author's plan, co-authoring the salvific story of his earthly journey and setting an example for every man and woman to follow.

Perceiving Christ's story in this way, we find a hermeneutical lens through which to make sense of our own lives and how we are meant to fit into God's cosmic story. In this cosmic story we have a perfect model for how the protagonist, Christ, dealt with the conflict arising from the workings of the antagonist, the devil. Rather than being a story divorced from our own, our individual life stories are meant to find their realization in Christ's story. It was Christ who modeled a perfect life of obedience to the Father. His was a life that accepted the Father's call to suffer on behalf of humanity, and due to Christ's perfect obedience to the Father's purpose, every soul might benefit and share in the glory Christ has now in the presence of the Father and the Holy Spirit.

Moreover, every individual's life appears to naturally parallel the three stages of the cosmic story. When comparing one's life to the grand story, we might interpret childhood as an individual's experience of humanity's state before the fall—that is, innocence in the presence of God. The age of reason is a sort of "fall" experience in which one begins to willfully choose evil and thus suffer separation from God. There might come a point when one encounters Christ and is forever changed, thereby personally experiencing the salvific event of history intended for all mankind. Like Christ, one may grow into deeper understanding of his or her story's purpose, realizing and living into a unique mission in implicit and explicit ways when the time is right. And just as humanity longed to return to its pre-fallen relationship with God, each individual has a sense of the good that must be recovered. An individual will look back to childhood as an ideal of the good to strive for, but he knows that he must press forward to fight for the good and to return home to God when his life is over.

The same pattern is apparent in both—an ideal state is lost and meant to be recovered. Just as in any story a conflict charges the protagonist with mission, in each of these romance stories the protagonist is charged with a mission to respond to the conflict. In the cosmic story of salvation history, Christ the protagonist receives the mission from the Father to redeem fallen humanity from the clutches of the devil. In each human story, one receives a personal mission from God to fight against evil and to defend and recover the good. The eschaton is the final destination of the cosmic story and each human story. When all things are revealed in the eschaton, it will become apparent how each human story fits into the cosmic story of salvation. Heaven might be perceived as the revelation of the grand storybook of creation, in which God, the best Author, assigned a unique role to each individual and masterfully interweaved every life story into a grand story. Hell, on the other hand, might be seen as a willful rejection of one's personal story, which is essentially a rejection of the grand story into which one was meant to fit.

CHILDHOOD
Childhood Innocence

From both his writings and the details of his personal life, we know that Chesterton idealized childhood as "a more real life" than adulthood.[2] Playing games, putting on plays in his toy theater, and entering into fairytales all symbolized the receptivity of childhood that allowed one to be oneself and see others for who they are. In fact, children appear to take themselves and others more seriously than adults in the sense that children put up no false appearances to mask their identity. Children receive

2. G.K. Chesterton, *The Autobiography of G.K. Chesterton*, in *The Collected Works of G.K. Chesterton* (San Francisco: Ignatius, 1988), 16:58.

every gift in trust, knowing that their parents will provide for them. Every detail of the world around has the sense of surprise and gift; the child perceives things with new eyes that have not grown weary. Chesterton remarks about these early years, "What was wonderful about childhood is that anything in it was a wonder. . . . It was a miraculous world."[3]

Childhood marks a time of performing simple activities as ends in themselves, conveying a sense of appreciation for the little details of life. Reflecting back on his childhood in his autobiography, Chesterton treats childhood play and crafts as more serious than adult work: "I wish we did not have to fritter away on frivolous things, like lectures and literature, the time we might have given to serious, solid and constructive work like cutting out cardboard figures and pasting coloured tinsel upon them."[4] He claims a few pages later in his autobiography that the puppet show *Punch and Judy* at his childhood home on Campden Hill meant more to him than the things he wrote as a journalist.[5]

What Is Lost

From various works of his, we might gather hints at what Chesterton believed to have been lost from childhood upon becoming an adult. For one, Chesterton perceives that adults easily lose the "eternal appetite of infancy" that capacitates one for seeing everything with wonder.[6] The child, free from society's expectations and lacking much life experience, does not grow bored at the repetition of the same game or seeing the same flower everywhere. Rather, children "exult in monotony"[7] because "mere life is interesting enough" for them.[8] To see things with wonder is to

---

3. Chesterton, 45.

4. Chesterton, 50.

5. Chesterton, 58.

6. Chesterton, *Orthodoxy*, 56.

7. Chesterton, 56.

8. Chesterton, 49.

see things as they are; realizing the divine origin of objects and people and the design behind them ought to evoke a sense of surprise that the Creator is perceivable in his creation.

This childlike way of seeing things as they are is what Chesterton calls "the unspoilt realism and objectivity of innocence."[9] Perhaps this is the primary virtue that is lost from childhood—clearly perceiving one's life and the world as they are. However objective their simple and unsullied perception may be during the first few years of life, children are typically unaware of the course their lives should take. Experiences are the normal means through which individuals gain clarity about their lives and the actions they should take; grace builds upon nature in a practical way. Nevertheless, with the fading of childhood, fantasies about one's life and false perceptions of oneself tend to arise due to voices other than God's. Though children would not realize their full potential if they could stay as children, perhaps they are in a better position to recognize that they have a God-given potential, because they see themselves clearly as loved and guided by authorities. Chesterton sums up the realism and self-awareness of children here: "I have never lost the sense that [childhood] was a more real life . . . that there was the white and solid road and the worthy beginning of the life of man; and that it is man who afterwards darkens it with dreams or goes astray from it in self-deception."[10] Even with experiences bringing clarity and drawing out one's potential, the matured individual must look back for an ideal of receptivity of meaning.

9. G.K. Chesterton, *The Everlasting Man*, in *The Everlasting Man: A Guide to G.K. Chesterton's Masterpiece*, ed. Dale Ahlquist (Elk Grove Village, IL: Word on Fire, 2023), 8.

10. Chesterton, *Autobiography*, 58.

Symbols in Chesterton's Childhood

An important observation to make from Chesterton's recounting of his childhood in his autobiography is the sense of allegory and symbolism in his early years. Symbolism seems to be a mark of divine influence and providence in one's story, whereby later in life one looks back on certain moments and realizes that God was working there and pointing to a future moment of grace he had in store. Writing his autobiography in the last year of his life, Chesterton realizes that moments and images in his childhood were a foretelling of his future: "Yet the landscape as I see it now, was not altogether without a visionary and symbolic character."[11] For Chesterton, the water tower near his childhood home was a symbol of his Baptism, which happened right down the street in St. George's Church.[12] He notes the fitting name of this church, since St. George was a key figure representing his romantic worldview, his love for his country, and the paradoxes of the Catholic Church whose doors he would one day enter.

Another example he provides is a childhood memory of someone painting the head of a white horse, a moment he connects with the white horse pub sign he saw years later on his honeymoon.[13] As an additional example, before their marriage, Chesterton proposed to his wife at the bridge of St. James's Park in London, which reminded him of the bridge to the princess' tower in his childhood toy theater collection (Figure 3).[14]

11. Chesterton, 38.
12. Chesterton, 38.
13. Chesterton, 43.
14. Chesterton, 151.

Figure 3. Photograph of a church tower from the toy theater collection. G.K. Chesterton Library, University of Notre Dame London Global Gateway, London, UK.[15]

Interestingly, Chesterton ends his autobiography with the same sense of allegory and symbolism with which he opened the account of his life. Suggesting that his own life was a "detective story . . . with its own particular questions answered and its own primary problem solved," Chesterton goes on to reveal the answer he found: "This overwhelming conviction that there is one key which can unlock all doors."[16] In case we are left wondering what he is referring to, Chesterton connects his entire

15. An archive-finding aid identified this piece as "a church, with statue in niche." It is not unlikely that Chesterton used this same piece as a princess tower, which would have appeared in various toy-theater plays and is symbolic of his childhood and his romantic worldview.

16. Chesterton, *Autobiography*, 331.

life together by connecting the key to life, what for him was the Catholic Church, to his very first memories of his toy theater, stating, "For me my end is my beginning."[17] Chesterton poetically ends his autobiography on a note of symbolism:

> And there starts up again before me, standing sharp and clear in shape as of old, the figure of a man who crosses a bridge and carries a key; as I saw him when I first looked into fairyland through the window of my father's peep-show. But I know that he who is called Pontifex, the Builder of the Bridge, is called also Claviger, the Bearer of the Key; and that such keys were given him to bind and loose when he was a poor fisher in a far province, beside a small and almost secret sea.[18]

This symbolic perception of life is characteristic of the Christian view of divine providence. First, recognizing recurring symbols throughout one's life is a great statement of faith that God acts in intentional ways whenever and wherever he wills to surprise us and to weave our lives together into a coherent narrative. It is a way of reverently treating God as the Author who intentionally places details in one's life and promises beautiful surprises to come in the future. Second, this symbolic approach is a way of perceiving one's life story as fully integrated in a way that it ought to be. Indeed, the cohesiveness of one's past, present, and future is a strong sign of the purpose of one's story. God's purpose for one's story is often expressed through recurring symbols, just as Chesterton retrospectively recognized his conversion to Catholicism to be apparent in the symbols of his childhood. Third, this approach confirms a point just made— namely, that life's experiences evince clarity about one's purpose,

17. Chesterton, 331.
18. Chesterton, 331.

79

containing symbols that appeared earlier in life. Even then, one must retain "the unspoilt realism and objectivity of innocence"[19] that allow one to see the symbols as they are, without skepticism and without superstition.

THE AGE OF REASON AND THE DEVIL

There comes an inevitable point early in life that every human soul must experience. The soul, at the waning years of childhood, enters into a new state of being marked by moral responsibility. Whether one recognizes it immediately as a sharp transition or retrospectively as a blurry dissolution, what is clear is that one knows he is now responsible for his actions in a way he might not have been during the first years of his life. This moment or period of transition during the fading years of childhood is known as the beginning of the "age of reason," and it certainly begins a new "age" in the sense of a lengthy span of time. In fact, what begins at the age of reason is a lifelong battle. From this point on, the soul recognizes that it cannot remain neutral between the good and evil sides it perceives around it. Perhaps even before the soul notices a transition has occurred, both good and evil are vehemently making a claim on it. A return to ignorance of one's responsibility is not an option. Now aware of good and evil, the soul feels the moral compulsion to choose which side to serve. The age of the lifelong battle has commenced.

Coming off the rosy years of childhood during which the inherent goodness of every created thing seemed inviolable, the young soul will have a first tangible experience of evil that seems to violate this precious existence. Attempting to make sense of this "enormous exception" of evil, it perceives a few options.[20] The earliest and easiest option is to dismiss this experience as a mistake and to return to childhood innocence. However, it

19. Chesterton, *Everlasting Man*, 8.
20. Chesterton, 407.

realizes this option is not possible; the encounter with evil was real, and it cannot erase this experience. Moving on to the second option, it may either invent or receive from others a "rudimentary philosophy" that explains the evil experience in relation to the authentic experience of good during childhood.[21] Knowing it cannot return to innocence, it might entertain the worldview that the evil experience was a mistake and that the good in this world is thoroughly inviolable. But this one experience of evil and the recurring threats to its own happiness are too real for it to dismiss optimistically. On the flip side, it may heed the voices that bemoan the impossibility of living a happy and good life. But it knows that the world is far too good to give credence to this pessimistic explanation. This young soul may consider other viewpoints accounting for good and evil, such as dualism or an a-religious theory denying the existence of evil. In the end, none of these theories provides a satisfactory explanation for what the soul perceives to be its own inherent goodness and the evil that is threatening it.

This scenario of the searching young soul is a real one—it is Chesterton's own experience, and it is one that can resonate with every soul. In his autobiography, Chesterton speaks to his own tangible experiences of evil during childhood before Christianity provided him with the answers he was looking for. In great contrast to the preceding autobiography chapter where Chesterton writes about his childhood, Chesterton's tone suddenly grows serious and compunctious as he recounts the dark years of his youth. He begins the chapter solemnly: "I deal here with the darkest and most difficult part of my task; the period of youth which is full of doubts and morbidities and temptations; and which, though in my case mainly subjective, has left in my mind for ever a certitude upon the objective solidity of Sin."[22] Although

21. G.K. Chesterton, *Where All Roads Lead*, in *The Collected Works of G.K. Chesterton* (San Francisco: Ignatius, 1990), 3:48.

22. Chesterton, *Autobiography*, 85.

Christianity would later provide him with explanations to dispel this confusion, Chesterton admits that he had a tangible experience of evil by his own doing. The danger his soul experienced is palpable when reading about his memory of this time: "But I am not proud of believing in the Devil. To put it more correctly, I am not proud of knowing the Devil. I made his acquaintance by my own fault; and followed it up along lines which, had they been followed further, might have led me to devil-worship or the devil knows what."[23] What was certain for Chesterton from this period of adolescence was that sin and the devil exist.

This experience of evil, which took Chesterton almost by surprise, compelled him to begin a search he had never anticipated. Leading up to those darker years, Chesterton admits his ignorance of the coming darkness and the search for an explanation: "At this time I did not even know that this morning light could be lost; still less about any controversies as to whether it could be recovered. . . . And as I did not foresee the problem I naturally did not foresee any of my searches for a solution."[24] With this experience in the background, the young Chesterton would search for years for a philosophy that defended the good and explained the evil without dismissing it. He found the pervasive attitude of pessimism to be "blasphemous" against the good of creation; at the same time, he found the cheery promise of optimism to be "false and disheartening."[25] In his adolescent years, Chesterton would come to create his own "rudimentary" philosophy of gratitude for existence,[26] one that during his adult years he would find supported and cultivated by the Christian tradition.

For the searching Chesterton, Christianity offered two firm doctrines that he found to best explain good and evil—the fall

23. Chesterton, 85–86.
24. Chesterton, 58–59.
25. Chesterton, *Orthodoxy*, 78.
26. Chesterton, *Autobiography*, 96.

and the existence of the devil. The doctrine of the fall was for him Christianity's more developed language for his own "Doctrine of Conditional Joy," which claimed that "an incomprehensible happiness rests upon an incomprehensible condition."[27] Chesterton's fairytale doctrine and Christianity's doctrine of the fall both asserted this core principle: one must not "resist any rule merely because it was mysterious."[28] Both in the garden of Eden and in daily life, God has established an objective moral order that must not be violated, even if its principles are mysterious. Applying this logic to one's life story, individuals will not perceive at once the full extent of the life God has in store for them. Yet their incomprehensible happiness, both present and future, depends on their obedience to the mysterious promise of an incomprehensibly joyful life. One's story is very prone to wanton influences; one's "happiness is bright but brittle" like glass.[29] The good news that Chesterton found in Christianity is "that to be breakable is not the same as to be perishable. Strike a glass, and it will not endure an instant; simply do not strike it, and it will endure a thousand years."[30] Before we take this image too literally in applying it to our lives, we might recognize that the glass *can* remain inviolate. Admittedly, however, the glass, which is our happiness and the state of our soul, is often cracked and shattered through external and internal acts of evil.

The other key answer that Chesterton discovered in Christianity is the assertion that the devil exists. Paradoxically, for Christianity to assert the existence of the devil is to assert good as primitive and antecedent to evil. Chesterton noticed in the creation account of Genesis the importance of the detail that God created all things as good. Following this point to its full implications, he realized its profound meaning: "It is the thesis

27. Chesterton, *Orthodoxy*, 52.
28. Chesterton, 53.
29. Chesterton, 52.
30. Chesterton, 52.

that there are no bad things, but only bad uses of things. If you will, there are no bad things but only bad thoughts; and especially bad intentions."[31] Even the devil and the other fallen angels were created good before their rebellion corrupted them morally. The essential point is that good is primitive and that evil is always parasitic on the good—it has no substance of its own.[32]

Interestingly, this principle has practical applications for how one understands the objectivity of his life story. It sets up a framework for discerning the Holy Spirit's inner working and the deceptions of the devil. The Holy Spirit affirms one's primitive goodness and encourages righteous intentions toward the development of one's story. On the other hand, the devil offers only a fantasy of the true self—what we can call the "ego"—which is in fact not one's true self but a false self. He lures one toward the building up of the ego, which will ultimately lead to rebellion against God and against one's true self. In the same way that the devil stirred up distrust of God's mysterious commandment not to eat the fruit (whether literal or metaphorical) of one particular tree in the garden of Eden, the devil seeks to stir up bad intentions in our own hearts against God's mysterious plan. Like the first humans who listened to that poisonous advice, when we concede, we find our happiness shattered, having abandoned God's plan.

The Enemy of Romance and Story

The devil is the antagonist and cosmic anti-patriot of God's story, as well as of every human story. Just as humanity, as a corporate whole, experiences the effects of the devil's primordial deception of our first parents, each person is born into this fallen, dysfunctional world with an enemy already committed to derailing his or her life story. This is the universal fate of mankind—that upon

31. G.K. Chesterton, *St. Thomas Aquinas*, in *The Collected Works*, 2:485.
32. Chesterton, *Everlasting Man*, 406–408.

reaching the age of reason, a soul enters into a lifelong battle against a vicious enemy, whether or not the enemy and battle are recognized. Thus, every life story contains this essential element of a battle against evil. It is important to clarify that evil is not inherent to the story, as if God could not write a story without evil; rather, the presence of evil is an effect of humanity's misuse of free will. Even with this seemingly unfortunate element of every story, the lifelong contention against evil gives rise to romantic elements of life, such as fighting for and loving the good, being fought for and loved by Christ, and embracing the adventure of avoiding danger in the pursuit of good. Being born into this fallen world casts us into the ring, challenging us to the lifelong duel of "wrestl[ing] with the devil, as every man must to be worth calling a man."[33] Though it is an objective struggle experienced by all, each struggle is personal and unique in its details, and through it one comes to find his dignity as created by God with a particular response to this fallen world.

Through various tactics, the devil seeks to disturb all of the elements that make the romantic story of life beautiful and exciting. First, the devil is against an adventurous and exciting life. This is a peculiar observation, because evil lifestyles often present themselves as more adventurous than holy lifestyles of prayer, chastity, temperance, and humility, all of which the culture would dismiss as boring and overly regimented. The devil convinces us that adventure arises from extravagantly exploiting the pleasurable things of life, constructing a grand narrative for oneself, and accruing masses of money to fund these endeavors. But Chesterton, echoing the paradoxical truths of the Beatitudes, reminds us that we can only receive adventures, not create them apart from God: "For an adventure is, by its nature, a thing that comes to us. It is a thing that chooses us, not a thing that we

---

33. G.K. Chesterton, *St. Francis of Assisi*, in *The Collected Works*, 2:102.

choose."[34] Wealth, power, honor, and pleasure are often treated as the means to adventures when too often they are hindrances to adventure. The devil would have us demand or even create adventures apart from God, but by demanding we miss out on the adventure given to us by God: "Adventures are to those to whom they are most unexpected—that is, most romantic. Adventures are to the shy: in this sense adventures are to the unadventurous."[35]

Second, and related to adventure, the devil is the enemy of thrift. As we have just seen, extravagance kills adventure because in having excess one is not in a position of receiving. The devil stirs up jealousy that others' lives are more adventurous than one's own. Instead of giving thanks for the particulars of one's life and committing to the adventure chosen for him, one may desire to have every other person's story. This results in the division of one's will among all these desires, preventing one from freely committing to the adventure given to him. Chesterton reminds us that "thrift is the really romantic thing" because "it is creative; waste is unpoetic because it is waste."[36] Waste results from desiring to live others' adventures; one's own adventure is lost, and one fails to gain the other adventures he demands.

Third, the devil is the enemy of fighting and loving. If love is understood to be willing and committing to the good of another, the devil is entirely uninterested in love and commitment. He abandoned the Creator in his primordial refusal to serve, and all of his evil works are ordered toward a refusal to commit to others. One way in which the devil incites this mentality is convincing us from time to time that we are not responsible for anyone else; their battle is their own. The problem with this mentality is that their battle is in fact our battle; their personal story is our story,

34. G.K. Chesterton, *Heretics*, in *The Collected Works*, 1:142–144.

35. Chesterton, 74.

36. G.K. Chesterton, *What's Wrong with the World*, in *The Collected Works of G.K. Chesterton* (San Francisco: Ignatius, 1987), 4:120–121.

and vice versa. God created each person with a special role to play in the grand story of creation, and nobody else can play that role in that way. To leave others to their own devices is to refuse the responsibility to love others and fight for their story, which is everyone's story. The heroes of the grand story will be those who fought and helped save others from the "dragons" in their lives. As Chesterton admitted, "I never had the slightest real doubt that heroes ought to fight with dragons."[37]

Fourth, speaking now to the elements of story, the devil abhors every detail of the grand story that he opted out of in his primordial rebellion. Since the devil is not God, he cannot create another story of the same grandeur. Forever jealous of this grand story that he chose not to participate in, the devil is committed to disrupting the details of the grand story and the human characters whom God created to live fully into this grand story. The devil notices that God's grand story of creation has perfect proportion, expressing the best elements of objectivity and subjectivity. The story has an objective goal of beatification and unification in God; even within this objective mission, free agents each bear subjective missions that are mini expressions of the grand objective. The devil seeks to disturb the objectivity of beatitude in God by convincing humanity to settle for happiness in created things; these express God's goodness, but they are not God. The devil tries to disturb one's unique mission by enticing one to live only for oneself, taking subjectivity too far. Ultimately, the devil can only divide up a story that he could not create.[38] The sad news is that desertion of the grand story is a possible option for humans, just as it was for the devil. But the overwhelmingly good news is that God's story is bound to be victorious over any damage caused by the story's antagonist.

---

37. Chesterton, *Autobiography*, 51.

38. G.K. Chesterton, *The Thing: Why I Am a Catholic*, in *The Collected Works*, 3:311.

Past Mistakes and Personal "Deaths"

A very important question is bound to arise from this consideration of the devil and our stories: "What is the role of sin in our stories?" If we understand sin as a rejection of the good, then every sin is a rejection of God, who is most good, and of his plan, which is abounding with good intentions and surprises. Any sin would be a hindrance to the ultimate goal of our stories—namely, beatitude and the fullness of joy in unity with God and humanity.

It also became evident earlier that evil is never a better option than good. An evil means never justifies a good end. This is the proper conclusion if evil is not primitive in creation but a result of a misused free will. If evil is never a proper means to a good end, how can evil ever contribute to the goodness of our stories? Additionally, sins have varying degrees of seriousness, with more serious sins being more capable of derailing one's story. We might begin to wonder if any sin could permanently derail the story we were meant to live.

These are huge questions with important implications for how we understand our lives, but the Christian understanding of salvation deals hopefully with these problems, which would be hopeless without a Savior. In the final chapter of *The Everlasting Man*, "The Five Deaths of the Faith," Chesterton seems to offer a hint for understanding how our stories might "die" in sin but how thereafter they come back to life because the author of our stories is divine and because this author knows "the way out of the grave."[39]

Chesterton proposes what he considers a more impressive theory about the Church's nature than the theory that the Church simply "survived" for two thousand years. More impressive than survival is revival.[40] Chesterton purports that the

---

39. Chesterton, *Everlasting Man*, 419.
40. Chesterton, *Where All Roads Lead*, 31.

Church actually experienced a "death" five times in its history; what he considers to be five major heresies ought to have interred the Christian faith forever, because they appeared more popular and truthful than orthodoxy. The irony is that the Church came back alive with greater strength and truth: "Christianity has died many times and risen again; for it had a God who knew the way out of the grave."[41]

Continuing to develop his theory of death and resurrection of the Church throughout history, Chesterton offers a brilliant claim consistent with the Catholic tradition—that the Church uses heresies toward the good of its tradition. Though the major heresies wounded the Church and painfully severed away impurities and evil, the Church would regain its vitality with greater self-understanding and strength. As Chesterton puts it, "And it always began by rejecting this old stone and ended by making it the head of the corner; by bringing it back from the rubbish-heap to make it the crown of the capitol."[42] It is paradoxical that the Church would work even a heresy into its foundation. But from the Arian heresy, which nearly entombed the Church forever, for example, the Church clarified its understanding of Christ as truly divine, a key dogma that Christians would forever be glad was defined.

Chesterton names two necessary conditions that have allowed the Church to rise from each of these historic deaths— the Church's truth and the divinity of its founder. Rightly put, the Church could only be "regularly recurrent under two conditions: first, that it was really true; and second, that the power in it was more than mortal."[43] Chesterton understood heresies to be "half-truths";[44] these half-truths may appear victorious over the whole truth for a time, but the Church as the bearer of the truth

41. Chesterton, *Everlasting Man*, 419.
42. Chesterton, 421.
43. Chesterton, *Where All Roads Lead*, 37.
44. Chesterton, 46–47.

would soon reappear after the half-truth died out. Moreover, Chesterton seems to make the case that the Church would not be around today if it were a merely human institution. The Church has a divine founder, and God will not let it succumb to permanent death. The Church is Christ's Mystical Body, which experiences the same fullness of death and life three days later experienced by the crucified and risen body of Christ that walked the earth two thousand years ago.

How does Chesterton's theory of the death and resurrection of the Church apply to our life stories and to sin? This theory about the Church accounts well for sins, which indeed cause deaths in our stories, and for salvation, which truly resurrects our stories. First, we must acknowledge that our spiritual lives and our stories are not flat narratives unaffected by sinful and righteous actions. Venial sins effectively distance us from God and the story he has intended for us to live. Mortal sins tragically divorce us from our Creator, and they have great potential for seriously derailing our stories. In rejecting the good through sin, we effectively deny God's story for us and forget who we were meant to be, having rejected the Author of our lives.

Despite the tragic reality that sins either venially or mortally wound our stories, great hope for the revival and recovery of our stories is founded upon two conditions—our story is true, and its Author is divine. No matter how far one has run from the divinely chosen narrative of his life, a spark of hope always remains, kindling in the recesses of his heart thoughts such as these: "I have forgotten who I am in my sin. I must return to the one who knows me best. He will remind me who I am and for what purpose he has created me." The dead soul retains in its inner core an undying ember that longs to reignite the soul into a blazing fire, vehemently knowing and proclaiming the purpose for which it was made. Though evil enjoyed its temporary triumph, the divine Author draws up the undying truth from within the soul, allowing its Creator to resurrect it.

The next point to realize is that resurrection does not erase the wounds of the past. Though sins can be forgiven and debts paid, their effects linger. But even the effects of sin are material for resurrection. To understand this further, we may look to the resurrected Christ, who appeared to the disciples in a glorified body that still bore the five wounds of the cross. Christ did not erase the marks of his shaming, torture, and death or pretend they did not exist. Christ did not reappear as a spirit but in the same body that bore the brunt of the world's evil. Though it may seem that extreme sins, such as ending someone's life, could permanently derail a story, even then God can work with these details because he is sovereign over his story and because his truth for each soul cannot permanently die to sin. In many cases, mortal wounds of the past become glorified wounds that show forth God's victory over death, just as Christ's wounds will forever manifest his eternal victory. For instance, some people who had taken another person's life have converted, using their dark pasts to defend and promote life through proactive education, testimonies, and prayer. If this were a purely human story, it should have ended in death and defeat long ago. But like the Church, our story is true and has a divine founder who "knew the way out of the grave."[45]

The Recovery of Innocence

As we have seen above, the age of reason marks the departure from childhood innocence and the beginning of a lifelong battle for good against ceaseless attacks. Having experienced evil as a shocking contrast to the goodness and purity of childhood, the soul longs to return to innocence. But the soul soon realizes it cannot simply retreat back to innocence; the only way back to innocence is to press forward through life. With the passing away of childhood comes the charging with responsibility to live

45. Chesterton, *Everlasting Man*, 419.

fully into one's story and to positively contribute to the stories of others. Having realized the assaults of evil against one's own story, others' stories, and the grand story comprised by these, one knows he cannot shirk his responsibility in a selfish return to the past. The quest for innocence will be a forward battle march that looks to the past as an ideal to strive for. He may even soon realize that his life story is a specific response to the world he was born into. Aware of the romance story prepared for him, he charges forth to welcome the adventurous life of recovering innocence, fighting for good against evil, and committing to the story through which he and others might reach full union with God once again.

CHAPTER 5

Story and the Paradox of Freedom

"Christianity is a superhuman paradox whereby two opposite passions may blaze beside each other."[1]

A DEFINITIVE PHILOSOPHICAL POSITION

Insofar as Chesterton's view of life as a story is a worldview—in the sense of a framework by which to make sense of all things—this view of life carries with it definitive claims and philosophical principles. The view of life as a story is, then, a philosophical position, one that has a logical approach to explaining human freedom, meaning, and purpose, just as other prominent philosophical positions like determinism or skepticism sought to do in Chesterton's time and to this day. To illustrate how inherent to the metaphor of story is a claim about freedom and meaning, we might consider the questions that naturally arise from viewing life in this way: If life truly is a story, then what details of the story has the divine Author already determined? If we are the co-authors, what details do we have the capacity to shape? If we are truly the characters and the co-authors who are free to co-author the story and to live out the narrative, how free are we?

---

1. G.K. Chesterton, *Orthodoxy* (Park Ridge, IL: Word on Fire Classics, 2017), 149.

Chesterton's Christian worldview has a methodology for addressing these foundational questions, which have practical implications for human happiness. But other philosophical positions likewise seek to answer the foundational questions about human freedom and meaning in this world. Determinism, depending on the form it takes, may conclude that the story of life is destined to end in a certain way and that human freedom (if it is granted at all) is ultimately powerless in determining the trajectory of the story. Existentialism may conclude that we are so free that we can create values for ourselves, calling that action "good" or that claim "true" to our liking. Skepticism may cast doubt on the existence of human freedom and meaning, concluding that this reality is an illusion.

What, then, distinguishes the Christian worldview from other philosophical positions, particularly with regard to human freedom and meaning? The Christian worldview does indeed have a definitive stance on human freedom, upholding it as a created, contingent reality that, despite being conditioned, nevertheless has a powerful capacity to order creation in a meaningful way—that is, aligned to the objective order of what is most good and most true. The Christian does not see himself as "free" to decide for himself apart from God what is good and true—that is not authentic freedom for the Christian, and it is both illogical and impractical to attempt to create a system of values misaligned with reality. However paradoxical it may seem, for Chesterton and for the Christian, the highest, most properly constituted form of freedom is to purposively order life according to God's objective order and to thereby discover the meaning behind the created order.

THE "BOTH/AND" PARADOX OF FREEDOM

Upon further consideration, it becomes more apparent that this Christian view of freedom, as evident in the view of life as a story, is most true to reality, accounting for freedom in a "both/and" paradoxical fashion. Let us consider the first paradoxical claim about human freedom—that freedom, properly understood, is inherently limited. As we have already seen in Chesterton's view of life as a story with romantic elements of thrift, to exercise the will is to embrace limitation; to choose one option is to decline the possibility of every other alternative. Rather than lamenting this fact as detracting from freedom, the Christian views this limitation as granting all the more seriousness and opportunity to every decision, for one must use his freedom wisely. In fact, it is precisely by operating within set bounds that freedom finds its full capacity to achieve a particular end. The artist is able to paint a house by drawing an object with a roof and walls, aligning to a particular pattern or form. The woman discovers her full capacity to be a wife and mother by committing herself to one family and one household, not to many families and many households. The artist and the wife become noble and praiseworthy by aligning and committing to the objectively valuable.

Freedom could also be said to be inherently limited in another sense—we cannot arbitrarily create values out of thin air, attributing goodness, truthfulness, beauty, and justice according to our liking. This fact arises from the reality that our freedom is created and contingent. God's freedom is capable of creating from nothing and ordering creation in a meaningful way, whereas we cannot create from nothing but can simply order creation in a meaningful way. It would be absurd for it to be otherwise—we could not call a murder inherently "good," a falsehood "true," a cacophonous clash of sounds "beautiful," and oppression "just." This is the position of the existentialist, who, as we will see further on, treats the will as the capacity to define for oneself what is true, good, beautiful, and just. By the existentialist's logic, anything can be meaningful, because anything could be good or true for that person. His meaning is without limits, except that his meaning is limited by its own absurdity.

Moreover, every philosophy that seeks to give an answer for human freedom must account for whether there is a divine will, and if so, what the relationship is between human freedom and divine freedom. Christianity answers this inquiry with another "both/and" paradox—God is fully free and humanity is fully free at the same time. The divine will and the human will are not in competition; the story of life is not a zero-sum game for the Christian. If God is truly the highest good, ordering all things toward the objectively best, then it follows that the best course of action is to align our will with the divine will. It still remains a free choice to align to what is most good and most true, but it would be unwise to choose otherwise.

Not surprisingly, other philosophies account for the divine will differently, either claiming it does not exist or, if it does exist, seeing it as mutually opposed to the human will. As existentialist philosopher Jean-Paul Sartre famously claimed in his work *Existentialism Is a Humanism* (1946), if God does not exist, we are free, and, alluding to Dostoevsky, "everything would be permitted." Sartre's logic is that if God *does* exist, then there is an objective order of values and meaning that we must align to, and therefore we are not free to create value and meaning to our liking. By taking on the view of freedom as the capacity to arbitrarily decide what is good and true and meaningful for oneself, we can only conclude that God's order is a threat to our freedom. But the validity of this view is contingent upon how we answer this question: Are we indeed free to create and assign value to our liking? If not, then we are on our way to seeing the relationship between human freedom and divine freedom as Chesterton would see it. To have an objective best to strive for, as well as full freedom to order our lives toward it, is the ideal for Chesterton and for the Christian, and to both of them it fortunately happens to be the case:

But in order that life should be a story or romance to us, it is necessary that a great part of it, at any rate, should be settled for us without our permission. If we wish life to be a system, this may be a nuisance; but if we wish it to be a drama, it is an essential. . . . A man has control over many things in his life; he has control over enough things to be the hero of a novel. But if he had control over everything, there would be so much hero that there would be no novel. . . . The thing which keeps life romantic and full of fiery possibilities is the existence of these great plain limitations which force all of us to meet the things we do not like or do not expect.[2]

POTENTIALITY AND ACTUALITY

Another paradox related to freedom—that even before we freely choose, the potential for the person we might become is all there—is captured in the old philosophical distinction between "potentiality" and "actuality" that Chesterton invokes to account for the determined and undetermined aspects of life. Chesterton attributes these notions to medieval Scholasticism in his book *St. Thomas Aquinas*, but John Henry Newman's idea of development, which took form a few decades before Chesterton's writing career, makes a similar point. Chesterton points out that many modern evolutionary determinists would at least "agree with Aquinas that there is everywhere potentiality that has not reached its end in act."[3] He continues, "But if it is a definite potentiality, and if it can only end in a definite act, why then there is a Great Being, in whom all potentialities already exist as a plan of action."[4] Chesterton and Aquinas agree with the determinists that everything is disposed toward a future state by

2. G.K. Chesterton, *Heretics*, in *The Collected Works*, 1:144–145.
3. G.K. Chesterton, *St. Thomas Aquinas*, in *The Collected Works of G.K. Chesterton* (San Francisco: Ignatius, 1986), 2:535–536.
4. Chesterton, 535–536.

virtue of potentiality, but to suggest that the future state is fated is to take potentiality one step too far.

Chesterton appeals again to medieval Scholasticism to complete his case about potentiality: "And there is an upper world of what the Schoolman called Fruition, or Fulfilment, in which all this relative relativity becomes actuality; in which the trees burst into flower or the rockets into flame."[5] Fruition here is the process by which something goes from potentiality to actuality. A familiar example used by Newman is that a seed has the potential to become a tree, but it must develop and unfold. Chesterton goes one step further to apply this claim about the development of Christian doctrine to his own life: "Now it may seem both a daring and a doubtful boast, if I claim that in my childhood I was all there."[6] He is not looking back at the end of his life and claiming that he was fated to become the writer, husband, and Catholic that he was. However, he does acknowledge in this passage that his childhood was filled with convictions and fundamental principles that disposed him toward future free decisions.[7] We catch a hint of this idea elsewhere when Chesterton claims that our lives are a story in which we are embarking on a mission to remember our own names that we once had but have since forgotten.[8] In these two examples of development and remembrance, we see an objective goal that is, in some form, present at the beginning.

This might be understood as "the paradox of the changing-stable self," in which one's potentiality unfolds into actuality under the workings of free will.[9] In his analysis of Chesterton's ontology, scholar Duncan Reyburn claims that being is not

5. Chesterton, 538–539.

6. G.K. Chesterton, *The Autobiography of G.K. Chesterton*, in *The Collected Works of G.K. Chesterton* (San Francisco: Ignatius, 1988), 16:57.

7. Chesterton, 57.

8. Chesterton, *Orthodoxy*, 50.

9. Duncan Reyburn, *Seeing Things as They Are: G.K. Chesterton and the Drama of Meaning* (Eugene, OR: Cascade Books, 2016), 101.

linear; one can know the final destination while also having the choice of how to get there.[10] This "subjectivity of objectivity" and "objectivity of subjectivity,"[11] which Reyburn hints at, can be found again in Chesterton's discussion on Aquinas. Chesterton offers what he calls "Thomist common sense" as an ideal accounting for the activity and passivity of the mind, an epistemological idea that has great relevance to this ontological discussion on determined and undetermined meaning.[12] According to Aquinas' philosophy, the mind is neither purely receptive nor purely creative. Rightly put, "this view avoids both pitfalls" in the sense that the mind neither receives exterior meaning that is already fully predetermined nor creates meaning and makes connections as if no meaning were already determined. Chesterton acknowledges that this philosophy is more practical and fruitful than the other extreme alternatives, because it is not a compromise but a paradox that brings the best out of passivity and activity in a way that the mind actually works.[13] He concludes, consistent with his romantic view of the world, that this "combination of an adventurous mind and a strange fact" is the reason for the thrilling nature of this paradox of freedom.[14]

These paradoxes that uphold both extremes simultaneously at their full strength—determinedness and un-determinedness, subjectivity and objectivity, potentiality and fruition, activity and passivity—are the core of our stories with regard to meaning and free will, and they find backing in Chesterton's writings. The fact that Chesterton views creation, life, and existence as a story and a work of art fashioned by the best author conveys his belief that this world has a design with intentional details, a plan of action, and a willful purpose. Even with the purpose already

10. Reyburn, 113.
11. Reyburn, 114.
12. Chesterton, *St. Thomas Aquinas*, 542.
13. Chesterton, 542.
14. Chesterton, 542; See also Chesterton, *Orthodoxy*, 3.

99

having been deliberately chosen and the objective standard of meaning already set, nothing is fated to happen because there exists a strange creative capacity called free will, a power that is "in its essence divine" and that allows man to creatively order the pre-established details and make connections in pursuit of the objective truth.[15]

Granted that a scale of meaning has already been determined, with a good analogy being the scale of morality, there may in theory be an objectively best story that one's life ought to take up. In this case, there might be an objectively best way the story ought to end—"happily ever after" or eternal life, for instance—as well as an objectively best plot or arrangement of details along the way. Even with this supposed objectivity, there are any number of subjective elements in which persons, the protagonists of their life stories, are able to willfully choose and participate in the details. There are any number of ways of getting to St. Louis from New Orleans, but some methods of travel and routes are easier or cheaper than others. Moreover, a person has potentiality from birth to become the best version of oneself, but the fruition or fulfillment of this potential occurs under the effects of exterior influences and willful choices. We might say that each story is directed toward a particular objective potential that is fulfilled under seemingly subjective circumstances. One may find solace in the proper proportions of passivity and activity, since one does not need to ceaselessly create meaning nor fearfully assimilate imposed meaning. These paradoxes can help present story as a realistic accounting of meaning and free will. This worldview acknowledges the high dignity of mankind by holding it worthy of an objectively best life story while allowing it to freely strive for this tangible goal.

15. Chesterton, *Heretics*, 142–144.

UNIVERSAL CALL: BEATITUDE

What, then, is the clear and tangible goal that Chesterton suggests is already set? He will suggest that it is beatitude, an objective that encompasses all other objectives. Beatitude, denoting "blessedness" and "happiness," is essentially synonymous with holiness and salvation, since salvation is to see the beatific vision in heaven and so to be supremely happy in the presence of God. It is a core tenet of Catholic belief that all mankind is called to holiness, salvation, and beatitude. Everyone's life stories, though so different from one another, ought to find unity in the universal call to holiness. In fact, everyone's life story ought to find unity in the fact that God is the one Author of them all. Like the books of the Bible, which together comprise the canon despite their striking differences in genre, authorship, and message, the unique stories of humanity ought to comprise and find unity in the storybook of creation written by the one divine Author. God is indeed the "one origin and one aim" of our stories, being the one "author" of them all.[16]

If we look more specifically to Chesterton to find this universal call to holiness and beatitude, we see that Chesterton states succinctly all that was said about the Catholic view of mankind's call to beatitude: "But for Catholics it is a fundamental dogma of the Faith that all human beings, without any exception whatever, were specially made, were shaped and pointed like shining arrows, for the end of hitting the mark of Beatitude."[17] He continues the simile, acknowledging the subjective element of free will amidst the objective purpose of beatitude, entirely consistent with the above discussion: "It is true that the shafts are feathered

---

16. G.K. Chesterton, *The Everlasting Man*, in *The Everlasting Man: A Guide to G.K. Chesterton's Masterpiece*, ed. Dale Ahlquist (Elk Grove Village, IL: Word on Fire, 2023), 259.

17. G.K. Chesterton, *The Thing: Why I Am a Catholic*, in *The Collected Works of G.K. Chesterton* (San Francisco: Ignatius, 1990), 3:150.

with free will."[18] Interestingly, in another book, Chesterton uses the same language of hitting the target, highlighting the romantic element of adventure and the subjective and objective elements of free will and design, respectively: "Exactly as a man in an adventure story has to pass various tests to save his life, so the man in this philosophy has to pass several tests and save his soul. In both there is an idea of free will operating under conditions of design; in other words, there is an aim and it is the business of a man to aim at it; we therefore watch to see whether he will hit it."[19] One thing is clear from this image—it is better to aim for and strike the target than not. As soon as the objectivity of hitting the center or the target itself is doubted, there is no longer a sport, because the thrill of practicing to accomplish a difficult goal is lost.

In addition to the target image, Chesterton expresses the objectivity of beatitude using language about being fully human. "Man is more himself, man is more manlike," Chesterton asserts as one of his dogmas, "when joy is the fundamental thing in him, and grief the superficial."[20] To put it even more colloquially, we might agree with Chesterton that we are just not ourselves and who we are meant to be when we are not joyful. Here again is an objective standard—mankind's potential is to be joyful and happy, a tangible purpose that anyone will admit to. Chesterton echoes this sentiment elsewhere in suggesting that humans, not animals, have a sense of their own potential: "Anybody might say, 'Very few men are really Manly.' Nobody would say, 'Very few whales are really whaley.'"[21]

However, the problem of problems that has filled literature and religion from the beginning is that achieving a complete and lasting state of joyfulness is impossible in this troubled life.

18. Chesterton, 150.
19. Chesterton, *Everlasting Man*, 409.
20. Chesterton, *Orthodoxy*, 162.
21. G.K. Chesterton, *The Blatchford Controversies*, in *The Collected Works*, 1:385.

Chesterton states the hopeful answer of Christianity, affirming mankind's potential for perfect blessedness, which strangely cannot come to full fruition in this life: "There is but one purpose in this life, and it is one that is beyond this life."[22] Chesterton masterfully closes out *Orthodoxy* with an allusion to this "gigantic secret of the Christian"—"joy," experienced in part in this life and fully in the next, because the Christian can know the One in whom we alone can achieve fulfillment. But Chesterton goes further to make an even more shocking claim—that Jesus' gigantic secret that he endeavored to hide his entire earthly life was his mirth, precisely because it would have been too wonderful to experience on this side of death. In the closing sentence of *Orthodoxy*, Chesterton puts it thus: "There was some one thing that was too great for God to show us when He walked upon our earth; and I have sometimes fancied that it was His mirth."[23] While on earth two thousand years ago humanity saw a sad, angry, or solemn Jesus, we can only imagine the mirthful Jesus that we will one day meet, whose joy would be too much for us to currently bear.

In sum, although we await the ultimate fulfillment of beatitude in the next life, while on earth we are still able to access and get a foretaste of the blessedness to come by living into the story that has beatitude as its destination.[24] Both the path and the destination of our life stories are rooted in the joy of God and humanity: "Life is a living story, with a great beginning and a great close; rooted in the primeval joy of God and finding its fruition in the final happiness of humanity."[25] Overall,

22. Chesterton, *St. Thomas Aquinas*, 481.

23. Chesterton, *Orthodoxy*, 164.

24. "Faith makes us taste in advance the light of the beatific vision, the goal of our journey here below. Then we shall see God 'face to face,' 'as he is.' So faith is already the beginning of eternal life" (*CCC* 163). We can sense the goal now; "already but not yet" do we experience the fullness of relationship with God. To a great extent, the fulfillment of one's purpose can happen while still on earth as our stories unfold.

25. Chesterton, *St. Thomas Aquinas*, 491.

these images are meant to assert beatitude as this one universal purpose of humanity, an objective purpose that plays out subjectively in individuals' stories, an objective that encompasses all other objectives, a potential that begins fruition in this life but achieves full actuality in the next.

ONE BEST LIFE?

With this extended discussion of free will and determinedness of meaning in the background, a vital question arises: "Is there one best life?" Many other questions are implicated in this central one—If there is one best life, how do we explain evil and suffering? Could a single mistake permanently prevent this one best life? How are we free to make this life our own if a certain path is already considered objectively best?

Before jumping to any sort of conclusion, it will be prudent to consider these implications and Chesterton's words, which may begin to hint at an answer. To claim a "best life" is to lay oneself and one's religious tradition open to strong objection. Voltaire's *Candide* is a famous objection to the tendency of Christians and Enlightenment rationalists to retreat to the principle that this world is the best of possible worlds, a claim asserted even in the height of natural disasters, wars, poverty, and other forms of mass suffering.[26] Christians, who often console afflicted friends and family by assuring them that "everything happens for a reason," are a hot target for Voltaire's invective.

However justifiable may be Voltaire's attack on the prevalent assumption of an objectively best reality, his satire tends to treat the flaws on the surface without raising a thorough argument against the logic of his opponents. One defense of the idea of a best life, including a life full of suffering or one

---

26. In various writings Chesterton flips this saying on its head, claiming that this is "the best of all impossible worlds" ("From the Note-books of G.K.C.," *The Tablet*, April 4, 1953, box 2, GKC Collection, 271). He uses the same wording in his book *Charles Dickens*.

ending prematurely, is that one's life is not isolated from those surrounding it. Voltaire overlooks the Christian claim—one that Chesterton's idea of story beautifully captures—that one's life is not one's own. Christians can believe with hope that suffering is redemptive for oneself and others. Suffering would be tragically vain if our lives did not bear upon one another and if this life did not bear upon the next. Thus, even suffering and an early death can become bearers of meaning since they may benefit the stories of others and since one's story is not annihilated at death.

Having proposed that the interconnectedness of lives can draw out the meaningfulness of suffering, we might consider if there is one best life and what free choice would look like in this case. First, to assert "one best life" is not to assume that this one possibility must happen, as if by fate or destiny. Chesterton expressly denies the notion of fate, which is counter to free will: "I deny (of course) that any human thing is destined to be anything."[27] Although not destined, the final destination of any individual is already chosen as best before he or she exists. The final destination is the same for every individual—union with God—but the path to this destination will look different and unique for each life that embarks upon the journey.

This point about unique paths of different individuals may be easily granted, but what about the many possibilities of life that someone could carry out? Chesterton affirms the previous point while also suggesting a great deal of choice between the lives one could live: "Every saint is a man before he is a saint; and a saint may be made of every sort or kind of man; and most of us will choose between these different types according to our different tastes."[28] Chesterton is a champion of the reality and efficacy of free will; free will is effective in changing the course of life and bearing upon one's eternal state, as established earlier. For

27. Chesterton, *Heretics*, 183.
28. Chesterton, *St. Thomas Aquinas*, 423.

Chesterton, free will is a "supernatural power of creation, as if [man] could raise the dead or give birth to the unbegotten."[29] Though appearing to give human freedom too much power, Chesterton understands free will to be a creative power on the order of secondary, not primary, causality. God creates from nothing and orders what he has created; man only orders what God has created. Thus, free will as the power to creatively order is a great responsibility laid upon man. In fact, Chesterton explicitly identifies free will as the "moral responsibility of Man."[30]

This connection between free will and moral responsibility is an entryway into understanding the responsibility to order every aspect of life according to an objective standard. Morality institutes an objective standard—some actions are better than others, good is better than evil, and everything falls in between. Some may object to the need to identify a "best," claiming that it is far more practical and immediate to seek a "better" option. While this is a good instinct, it only defers the question about the "best." For "it is impossible even to say that the change is for the better, unless the best exists somewhere, both before and after the change."[31] The comparative implies the superlative, the standard against which improvement and progress are judged.[32] While it may seem impossible to ever know the "best" with clarity, Christians can have a sense of it. Being in relationship with God, who is the "best" and the "highest good" (*summum bonum*) against which all subordinate goodness is judged, Christians can have a sense of the right direction as God calls them to himself by their own unique paths.

Having argued for an objective scale of morality and meaning, the next step in this argument is to establish that some uses of things in this life—including talents, lifestyles, relationships,

29. Chesterton, *Everlasting Man*, 402.
30. Chesterton, *St. Thomas Aquinas*, 435.
31. Chesterton, 535–536.
32. Chesterton, *Heretics*, 52.

intellect, money—are better than others. For instance, developing one's musical ability or pursuing deeper understanding in a field of knowledge is better than neglecting these opportunities out of laziness. What is key to this argument is that these materials of life are unique to an individual and are chosen by God with artistic attention to the details; every detail of who a person is—the family one is born into, one's propensities toward developing talents, etc.—express the purpose of God, who created each person with divine intentionality. If the details have the ultimate purpose of leading us to blessed union with God, and if the materials of life are the very means by which we are to reach this destination, then we have a moral responsibility to utilize our free will, this creative power of ordering, to order the materials of our lives according to the life path that is most conducive to the final destination of beatitude. The choice among types of lives to which Chesterton was referring is, then, not an arbitrary decision among equal options but one driven by a moral force. Each of us would be right to ask God: "How *ought* I to be living? What would *you* have me do?" If we perceive the moral force as a compulsion to be truly happy, then we might gladly welcome that single choice, which was what we were longing to choose anyway.

ORTHODOXY
The Three Ideals

Much remains to be said about the theory of one best life, but it will be beneficial to present specific illustrations of the above arguments about meaning and free will—that is, the determinedness and un-determinedness of life.

In "The Eternal Revolution," chapter 7 of *Orthodoxy*, Chesterton tells of three ideals that he had demanded for this life, and all three of them he found contained and cultivated by the Catholic Church:

I had said, "The ideal must be *fixed*," and the Church had answered, "Mine is literally fixed, for it existed before anything else." I said secondly, "It must be *artistically combined*, like a picture"; and the Church answered, "Mine is quite literally a picture, for I know who painted it." Then I went on to the third thing, which, as it seemed to me, was needed for an Utopia or goal of progress. And of all the three it is infinitely the hardest to express. Perhaps it might be put thus: that we need *watchfulness* even in Utopia, lest we fall from Utopia as we fell from Eden.[33]

Chesterton's three ideals are fixedness, or what we might call determinedness; artistic composition, which expresses the ideas of design, proportion, intentionality, and divine purpose; and watchfulness, which we might understand to be undeterminedness, since the fixed purpose will not happen automatically without the ordering power of free will.

These three ideals, which are consistent with earlier arguments about meaning, free will, romance, art, and story, are the ideals of Chesterton's worldview. First, viewing life as a story expresses elements of fixedness—the human person is created to reach the best possible destination, full union with God in the next life. Second, a story manifests artistic composition—God the Author and Artist has made intentional decisions in choosing the details with which to compose the story of one's life. Lastly, one's life story requires watchfulness—far from being fated, one's union with God requires a constant act of the will and a vigilant ordering of life's events and details toward the good.

The Familiar and Unfamiliar

Speaking to Chesterton's book *Orthodoxy* as a whole, one of the main messages of *Orthodoxy* is the two-fold human desire for

---

33. Chesterton, *Orthodoxy*, 114 (emphasis added).

determinedness and un-determinedness in life. In the opening chapter, in which he lays out the purpose for his book, Chesterton professes that the Christian faith has provided an answer to "this *double spiritual need*, the need for that mixture of the *familiar* and the *unfamiliar* which Christendom has rightly named *romance*."[34] Notice the vital connection that Chesterton is making. Very much consistent with the previous argument about his three ideals, Chesterton grounds his defense of Christianity in the "mixture of the familiar and the unfamiliar," a human need and demand that the romance of Christianity satisfies. This need is for determined and undetermined elements in life, not simply one of them in full force but a capacious coexistence in which neither loses its unique essence and power.

Chesterton's statement is a reiteration of the paradox of human and divine freedom—the unique life to which each person is called by God is one of great divine chosenness and simultaneously one of great opportunity to freely order the details, materials, and circumstances that God has intentionally chosen. We humans fiercely demand the settledness of truth and meaning; at the same time, we demand the elements of surprise and adventure that arise from unsettledness. Chesterton is not theorizing as an armchair philosopher; the very people he knew personally and saw walking the streets of London had expressed this double need: "But nearly all people I have ever met in this western society in which I live would agree to the general proposition that we need this life of practical romance; the combination of something that is strange with something that is secure."[35] Quite characteristic of Chestertonian paradox, we demand both extremes at their full force: "We want not an amalgam or compromise, but both things at the top of their energy."[36]

34. Chesterton, 2 (emphasis added).
35. Chesterton, 3.
36. Chesterton, 91.

The product of coexisting determinedness and un-determinedness, of familiarity and unfamiliarity, is the romance of life. And the romance of life is none other than a grand, adventurous story that God has chosen in his providence for each of us to freely live into. It is a life full of surprises, twists, and turns that one could never expect. Even then, we can trust that the unfolding events of life are ordered toward our desire for beatitude—the ultimate end of union with God. All in all, the romance of life is nothing less than our ultimate objective.

CHAPTER **6**

Fictional Illustrations
The Surprise *and* The Man Who Was Thursday

"According to most philosophers, God in making the world enslaved it. According to Christianity, in making it, He set it free. God had written, not so much a poem, but rather a play; a play he had planned as perfect, but which had necessarily been left to human actors and stage-managers, who had since made a great mess of it."[1]

THE SURPRISE

Chesterton's play *The Surprise* is perhaps the best extended fictional illustration of the demand for determinedness and un-determinedness in life. The ideas behind this play are not limited to this one work of his; in fact, *The Surprise* is in many ways an enactment of Chesterton's principles that he expresses in other works. In *Orthodoxy*, we can get a foretaste of this play, which Chesterton would write twenty-four years later: "According to most philosophers, God in making the world enslaved it. According to Christianity, in making it, He set it free. God had written, not so much a poem, but rather a play; a play he had planned as perfect, but which had necessarily been left to human actors and stage-managers, who had since made a great mess of it."[2] Additionally, *The Surprise* drives home Chesterton's principle

---

1. G.K. Chesterton, *Orthodoxy* (Park Ridge, IL: Word on Fire Classics, 2017), 76.
2. Chesterton, 76.

expressed in *Orthodoxy* that "the chief pleasure is surprise,"[3] in that humble receptiveness is a necessary ingredient for enjoying creation: "It is impossible without humility to enjoy anything—even pride."[4]

As for the story itself, it will be beneficial to give a general outline of *The Surprise* in order to highlight a few key points. The main characters are a traveling playwright called "Author," a Franciscan called "Friar," and many minor characters who are wind-up marionettes within Author's play—Captain, Guard, Poet, Princess, Maria, and King. *The Surprise* consists of two parallel acts that are plays within the play. In the first act, Author expresses to Friar that he must make his confession to him in the form of his play. Author winds up his marionettes to perform his play as he intended. A surprise occurs in which Princess, out of good will, arranges a marriage between the King and Maria, an outcome that fulfills everyone's desires. This first of two plays is "not only very short, but very simple."[5]

Having shown his play, Author confesses to Friar that he wrote this play for a bet; another "itinerant artist" had challenged Author that he could not write a play without villains.[6] This first play indeed wins the bet; the complex characters act virtuously and devise an exciting story, all without the need for villains or wrongdoing. But Author feels guilty that the simplicity and brevity of the plot do not do justice to the complexity of his characters, who he knows are "capable of a thousand other things besides the things they have to do on this stage."[7] Author is dissatisfied that they do right because this makes for a short

3. Chesterton, 26.

4. Chesterton, 27.

5. G.K. Chesterton, *The Surprise*, in *The Collected Works of G.K. Chesterton* (San Francisco: Ignatius, 1989), 11:302.

6. Chesterton, 321.

7. Chesterton, 322.

and simple story, but at the same time, he does not want them to do wrong.

During Author's long, heated soliloquy, Friar prays to God, and a miracle ensues in which the marionettes come to life; Author's play now becomes "their play."[8] Now alive with free will, the marionettes enact the play again, for the most part carrying out the same story but being more lifelike and altering some details of the play. However, instead of only acting virtuously, toward the end, the characters begin to quarrel, and violent threats ensue. Right when swords begin to clash, Author's head breaks into the play, ending the second play with exasperation: "And in the devil's name, what do you think you are doing with my play? Drop it! Stop! I am coming down."[9] Chesterton ends *The Surprise* with this strong allusion to the Incarnation, leaving the reader to imagine how Author would recover his story.

The Surprise contains many points of interest, some of which will be addressed here as relevant to free will and meaning. In interpreting this play, we must not take the words and actions of the characters to be direct and flawless expressions of Christian theology, but this form of representation is meant to aid consideration of Christian truths. Though much can be said about this play, the dialogue between the two main characters is of most interest to this discussion.

A first thing to notice is the connection between "Author" and God and the connection between the "itinerant artist" and the devil. Author declares himself to be the "Master Puppet-Maker of the World."[10] Like God, who writes the stories of humanity, Author proclaims, "What scenery there is, I paint. What plays there are, I write. I make them all and the story for which they are made."[11] As scholar Duncan Reyburn rightly

8. Chesterton, 325.
9. Chesterton, 340.
10. Chesterton, 300.
11. Chesterton, 300.

points out, Author's awareness and intentionality regarding his characters signify how God knows the potential and complexity of creation before it is made.[12] The challenge between Author and the itinerant artist suggests that God can indeed create an interesting story with only virtue and goodness; evil is not necessary for drama and excitement, as Reyburn highlights in his interpretation of this play.[13]

Second, Author's anxiety about the first play and his unwillingness to sacrifice his plan can shed light on God's willingness to "risk" his master plan for creation. Although God did not struggle or feel anxiety about giving free will to humanity, we humans may realize through Author's emotions and the two different acts how incredible a gift free will is; it is a power of secondary causality that reflects God's own power of primary causality. Although human freedom is quite limited compared to divine freedom, it somehow can alter the story that God had intended for humanity. Fortunately, though, God will not abandon the story to humans who could never on their own carry out a purpose that originated from a divine being. As the incarnational finish to *The Surprise* suggests, God is able to come down as one of us and rework the story from within.

Finally, one other point that can be drawn from the text is that divine surprise is superior to human surprise. The surprise of the arranged marriage in the first play is wrought by the character Princess; the surprise is grand and pleasing to all the characters, but Author is dissatisfied with the simple plot, even though the surprise causes a happy ending. The second play manifests the same attempt of surprise through the arranged marriage, but now that the characters have free will and the potential to act unvirtuously, the same surprise that impressed the characters in the first play upsets the same characters in the second play. Right

12. Duncan Reyburn, *Seeing Things as They Are: G.K. Chesterton and the Drama of Meaning* (Eugene, OR: Cascade Books, 2016), 95.

13. Reyburn, 81–82.

when the reader thinks that *The Surprise* is simply about two parallel surprises of arranged marriage, another surprise at the end shocks both the reader and the characters—Author comes down to save his play in a way that alludes to the Incarnation. In reading this insightful work of Chesterton, we might come to admit that God's surprises outweigh our own surprises, which cannot fully satisfy apart from him.

THE MAN WHO WAS THURSDAY

In addition to his play *The Surprise*, Chesterton's metaphysical thriller novel *The Man Who Was Thursday* can be interpreted as revealing profound philosophical truths. Chesterton published this novel in 1908 under the full title *The Man Who Was Thursday: A Nightmare.* This was the same year that Chesterton published his great apologetical work *Orthodoxy*, which marked a confident presentation of his belief in the Christian creed and the multiple influences and worldviews that led him there. The novel's subtitle, "A Nightmare," suggests a sort of dystopian setting, and Chesterton himself even claimed later in life in his autobiography that this novel was not meant to be a direct allusion to Christian theology.[14] That said, it is unsurprising that even a wild fictional romance of Chesterton's would be laden with philosophical dialogues, profound paradoxes, and strangely symbolic details that leave the reader wondering what Chesterton was implying with each mark of the pen. It is through this lens that this novel can be viewed as intentionally illustrative of Chesterton's worldview, both in its minor details and in its overall trajectory, even if Chesterton was not intending to draw a perfect parallel between the fictional story and Christian truths in every detail.

14. G.K. Chesterton, *The Autobiography of G.K. Chesterton*, in *The Collected Works of G.K. Chesterton* (San Francisco: Ignatius, 1988), 16:103.

Much can be said about the entire novel, from its iconic plot to its many memorable exchanges between the main characters. But what is of greatest relevance to this discussion is the ending of the novel, where the entire plot turns on its head in classic Chestertonian style and the meaning of the story becomes most apparent.

To first offer a brief summary of the work leading up to the final chapters, the novel begins in nineteenth-century England with an exchange between two poets, Gabriel Syme and Lucian Gregory. Syme is an undercover policeman on the side of order, while Gregory is on the side of anarchy. The antipodes of order and anarchy set up the central conflict for the remainder of the book. Gregory invites Syme to an underground anarchist meeting upon Syme's promising that he will not disclose their movement. Then Syme proposes to reveal his own secret to Gregory after receiving Gregory's promise to keep it secret, upon which Syme reveals his identity as an undercover policeman and Gregory becomes furious.

During the undercover anarchist meeting, the anarchist group—which it turns out consists of individuals with codenames for each day of the week—sets out to vote in a new member to serve as Thursday. In an ironic turn of events, Syme, the undercover policeman, offers a thunderous speech winning over the favor of the council, who collectively decides to vote in Syme as Thursday rather than Gregory.

The remainder of the story involves a mission charged to the anarchists by the leader of the group, Sunday—the task of blowing up Paris. Syme, as the undercover policeman, sets out to stop the other anarchists from carrying out the mission, only to discover, one by one, that each anarchist member is actually an undercover policeman spy on the side of order. Near the end of the story, the six council members ally themselves against the monstrous Sunday, the mastermind behind the destructive mission. Through a wild series of events, they chase Sunday through the English countryside only to be invited by an attendant to a banquet hosted by Sunday.

The six arrive to the banquet, where elaborate costumes are awaiting them, symbolizing the seven days of creation, with Syme—who was Thursday—donning an outfit with a sun, moon, and stars to symbolize their creation on the fourth day in Genesis. Outdoors, crowds of banquet-goers are dancing with merriment, each wearing a fanciful costume of various animals or manmade objects—birds, lampposts, and other creatures and items.

Both perplexed at the strange scene and strangely pleased by the atmosphere, the six men approach seven thrones gathered under the starlight to take their seats, with a vacant central chair awaiting Sunday's arrival. Sunday finally appears, dressed in a white robe and with gray-fire hair, taking his seat with an air of solemn reticence. The six begin to question Sunday what this entire anarchist mission meant, as well as why they suffered so much in this farcical, almost twisted, series of events, as if they were pawns in Sunday's game of chess. Sunday remains solemnly silent until the sudden arrival of Gregory, described as arriving in an all-black outfit and having fiery red hair—the real anarchist. Gregory verbally attacks the seven for not suffering the way he had, echoing the earlier questions of the six toward Sunday for why all these events happened the way they did. The climactic scene ends with Sunday finally speaking up, supposedly offering an answer to the six and Gregory for why they all suffered: "Can ye drink of the cup that I drink of?"[15] The setting suddenly shifts, as if waking from a dream, to Syme walking with Gregory, with the novel ending similarly to how it began.

Now considering how *The Man Who Was Thursday* evinces Chesterton's worldview that this life is a story and all the related

---

15. G.K. Chesterton, *The Man Who Was Thursday* (San Francisco: Ignatius, 1999), 263.

philosophical principles that this worldview upholds, Chesterton's choice of the word "nightmare" for the subtitle of this novel is a very peculiar one. Many readers and scholars of Chesterton have mused about the meaning behind this strange subtitle, but I would like to propose a way of interpreting this subtitle in an ironic sense that reveals a deeper meaning beyond the book and is consistent with Chesterton's worldview on display in his other works. The interpretation can be stated simply as this: Life can appear to someone as a nightmare if a higher power is manipulating the world against him, leaving him feeling "outplayed" by a stronger player or even as a pawn in some higher being's chess game. So it is for those whose worldview construes God—or some impersonal force like karma or fate—as ultimately against them or, at best, coldly neutral and indifferent. In the novel, the mastermind behind the story's plot, Sunday, is described throughout as a monstrous man, not only in size but also in presence. Each of the six philosophers claimed to have a different perception of Sunday, with all the others being surprised when Syme admits that Sunday's face, once he saw it, struck him as "so beautiful, because it was so good."[16] Further contributing to this sense of the nightmare, at the end of the novel when the seven are sitting on their thrones, Sunday, dressed strangely symbolically as God the Father in bright white, is reticently sitting on the central throne, almost to the point of being aloof from the demands from the six that Sunday explain himself. Up to this point, the six have felt frustration at Sunday for making them actors in his farcical play, and all for what?

But Sunday's single-sentence response that ends the scene is the key for understanding the novel's subtitle differently. Sunday suddenly addresses the six and Gregory with a powerful yet personal allusion to the suffering of Jesus, offering the sense that he had been attentively listening to their complaints the entire time

16. Chesterton, 246.

and leaving little need for them to respond: "Can ye drink of the cup that I drink of?"[17] In light of Sunday's response, Syme's earlier feeling that Sunday was benevolent and well-intentioned—which was impossible for the other five to fathom—suddenly becomes a possible position. Syme's worldview makes room to construe Sunday as a benevolent orchestrator of their plot. How the other five construe their final encounter with Sunday the reader does not get to learn, but the reader can leave off wondering how their encounter might have changed their perception of the mastermind behind it all.

This leads to the next observation: just as life can appear to someone as a nightmare when a higher power is seen as manipulative or cold, life can conversely appear to another as a dream—in the sense of a positive state that one does not want to end—when a higher power is seen as benevolently involved. This comparison of a personal worldview to a nightmare or dream is an insightful one. When you are asleep, a pleasant dream is always more desirable than a nightmare, but you cannot even by a strong act of will change a nightmare to a dream. Just so, the powerlessness of adjusting one's sleeping state is somewhat akin to the difficulty of changing one's worldview. People's worldviews are deeply embedded, and unless they have a reason to adjust their worldviews, they will have a preference to preserve and defend a network of connections that years of personal experiences have constructed. A mere act of will—however intentional it may be—is often not strong enough to change one's worldview. To take a real-life case of someone at an existential fork in the road, an agnostic may have had plentiful positive experiences of Christians and want to believe in the Christian God. But what is most likely is that the agnostic feels held back by a web of past convictions that an act of his own human volition cannot break him out of. Something more powerful is needed,

17. Chesterton, 263.

like an encounter with God or an "aha!" moment that Christians might call being gifted with faith. However it may happen, a truth is apparent from these real-life experiences and also within Chesterton's novel: it is most often the case that to change your worldview, something or someone more powerful than you must break through and challenge the way you construed the world.

To the resistant victim, such a challenge to one's worldview is an unwelcome affront. Most humans—as sinners, and even naturally as creatures of habit—are resistant victims. To every Christian who has encountered God, grace is an invasion, and God is anything but aloof or indifferent—he wants, if it can be put this way, to destroy the old order; he is preparing a plot to blow up Paris. Like the six policemen in the novel, the experience of being part of God's destructive plot can be nightmarish for the one experiencing it. It seems as if you are not in control; suddenly every detail of life takes on an appearance of working against you; you feel your deepest convictions being smashed and overwhelmed by amassing evidence against them; the mastermind behind it all (you might imagine) is laughing at you as he awaits your surrender; and when you get a word with the mastermind you will force him to explain the reason for this pain-filled plot.

However, when God breaks through, everything can look very different rather quickly. During his first few views of Sunday, Syme had only seen his back, and without a direct encounter, Sunday struck him as a dreadful man. But upon seeing his face later on, Syme's entire view of the mastermind suddenly changed. And with Sunday's remarks at the end of the novel, the entire plot takes on a completely converse interpretation. What if Sunday, in perhaps the strangest and most ironic way possible, was working all things for their good? What if they were not the objects of his joke but the subjects of a thrilling adventure that ends with the happy accident—or purpose—that they were all unknowingly conspiring for the same noble purposes of defending order? And what if, in an even wilder way, Sunday was bringing order to their own lives, somehow tricking them into achieving their own goals?

This is the revelatory truth that Chesterton gets at through this fictional story. God performs an entirely unforeseen sleight-of-hand maneuver, outdoing us, all ultimately for us and with our participation. In the moment, the 3D chess game feels like cruel deception, but at its achievement, it is revealed as an entirely intelligent and all-good magic trick that leaves us speechless.

This leads into another observation and principle of Chesterton's Christian worldview—everything will come full circle, and the purposes of the mastermind will all make sense in the end. The belief that "everything will work out in the end" may seem like a cliché that most people hold, but in our secular society, it is rather a profound act of Christian hope that is rarely found. Gregory, the true anarchist, and even the six policemen on the side of order desperately question Sunday on all of his purposes, wanting to know "why." But the question of "why" is in fact an affirmation that the story had a purpose that had to be discovered. One of the six, Friday, even questions Sunday why he "let [him] stray a little too near to hell."[18] So it is that we all wish to know "why" from God, even why he would let some of us stray so far into destruction just to bring us back to himself. The response of Sunday, which is more of a mysterious question than an immediately satisfying answer, provides a window into the logic of God. The suggestion, as Chesterton ponders in another work, is that even for someone at the extreme of human suffering and godforsakenness, God, through a seeming sleight-of-hand maneuver, has already beat him there.

Finally, a slightly different interpretation on the antipodes of anarchy and order in the novel can reveal a truth about philosophical worldviews that will be explored hereafter—namely,

18. Chesterton, 260.

that bad worldviews are truly destructive to human happiness. In the novel, Chesterton presents the six policemen not so much as armed forces that would restore order through physical force but as policeman "philosophers" who are hunting out dangerous worldviews. This detail is a core principle of Chesterton's, who deeply believed that one's worldview matters and that it has very practical implications on even mundane human activities, like giving gifts at Christmas. For Chesterton, a plot to blow up Paris is a very logical outcome of a destructive worldview, just as Chesterton predicted Nietzsche's insanity from a mile away, diagnosing his end condition based on his philosophical principles.

One's worldview is the most important thing that Chesterton wished to know about a person, not simply out of curiosity but because it said everything about who that person was, how they spent their time, what they valued, and quite truthfully how happy they were. For Chesterton, a worldview was not like a taste or opinion, which can rightfully vary and touch on only one aspect of life. Instead, a worldview was the deepest thing about a man, and it determined many things and meant everything. And far from being subjective, Chesterton had a deep conviction that there was an objectively "right" worldview, even if this right worldview is subjectively experienced and held across myriads of individuals. It is these truths about philosophical worldviews that we will now explore in the remaining chapters.

PART II

The Four Worldviews

CHAPTER 7

The Polarities of Subjectivity and Objectivity Across Worldviews

"A stick might fit a hole or a stone or a hollow by accident. But a key and a lock are both complex. And if a key fits a lock, you know it is the right key. . . . But a man is not really convinced of a philosophic theory when he finds that something proves it. He is only really convinced when he finds that everything proves it."[1]

INTRODUCTION

Up to this point, we have considered in great detail the shape, principles, and applicability of Chesterton's worldview—that life is a story. Chesterton's worldview is quintessentially a Christian worldview. Even more, this deeply Christian worldview held by Chesterton is not a deeply held religious conviction irrelevant to non-Christians, but rather a fiercely serious philosophical position that asserts (as any serious philosophical position would) that it is right about reality on the most foundational principles. Take any of Chesterton's major claims about his view of life as a story and trace it back to its premises, and it becomes clear how this worldview takes a definitive stake on core philosophical

---

1. G.K. Chesterton, *Orthodoxy* (Park Ridge, IL: Word on Fire Classics, 2017), 81.

principles, particularly on human freedom and our capacity to order life in a meaningful way.

Consider Chesterton's contrasting of a fatalistic philosophy with the Christian view of life as a story: "To the Buddhist or the eastern fatalist existence is a science or a plan, which must end up in a certain way. But to a Christian existence is a story, which may end up in any way."[2] The Christian philosophy, against the persistent strain of determinism in every age, upholds not only the existence of human freedom but also its capacity to shape the trajectory of the story and to make life meaningful in cooperation with God. Or, returning to Chesterton's example of a romantic adventure story and its likeness to hitting a target: "Exactly as a man in an adventure story has to pass various tests to save his life, so the man in this philosophy has to pass several tests and save his soul. In both there is an idea of free will operating under conditions of design; in other words, there is an aim and it is the business of a man to aim at it; we therefore watch to see whether he will hit it."[3] Here, Chesterton again affirms the existence of free will, but a strong element of objectivity is apparent in addition to the subjective use of the will. The fierce philosophical claim is that subjectivity must operate within the framework of objectivity. While subjectivists or relativists will try to deny the bounds of objectivity, Chesterton would argue that it is a philosophical necessity that subjectivity operate within objectivity. It could not be otherwise; even the claim "All meaning is relative" is an appeal to objective principles. But the fact that subjectivity must operate within objectivity is good news, because the objective is a source of order and "superlativity." Without objective order, we would not know what is most good, most noble, or most true to strive for.

2. Chesterton, 137.

3. G.K. Chesterton, *The Everlasting Man*, in *The Everlasting Man: A Guide to G.K. Chesterton's Masterpiece*, ed. Dale Ahlquist (Elk Grove Village, IL: Word on Fire, 2023), 409.

If the key question up to this point has been "What is G.K. Chesterton's worldview, and what are its philosophical principles on freedom and meaning?" the key question hereafter is "How does Chesterton's worldview stand up against other dominant philosophical positions on freedom and meaning, and which worldview is ultimately most true to reality?" To the extent that we wish to know which worldview is most correct, we will need to consider the core claims and principles of each dominant philosophical position, as well as their applicability to life, their limitations, and their end destination if their principles are carried out.

But before naming these dominant worldviews and exploring their positions on freedom and meaning, a more fundamental question must be addressed: Why does it even matter how each person views the subjective and objective, the undetermined and determined, freedom and meaning? Surely, the average person does not think of life in these terms anyway, and even if they do, why does their view of the world matter for them or anyone else? The answer is quite simple—because everyone has a view on what is subjective and what is objective (even if they do not use those terms), and this view undergirds every decision and every thought about what in life has value. And because of the intricate ties between one's worldview and every act and thought, it directly impacts one's happiness and determines the course one's life takes.

Chesterton knew this truth most keenly, claiming, "We have a general view of existence, whether we like it or not; it alters or, to speak more accurately, it creates and involves everything we say or do, whether we like it or not."[4] The applicability of one's worldview is nothing less than universal; nothing in life goes untouched by one's worldview. Additionally, if there was anything that Chesterton wished to know about someone, it was that

4. G.K. Chesterton, *Heretics*, in *The Collected Works*, 1:205.

person's worldview, as it reveals everything about him, not just how he thinks but also how he makes practical decisions: "But there are some people, nevertheless—and I am one of them— who think that the most practical and important thing about a man is still his view of the universe."[5] How someone spends an hour of free time or treats a waiter at a restaurant—these everyday practical decisions are all dictated by one's worldview.

THE FOUR WORLDVIEWS

Now, while everyone has his or her own subjectively held worldview, people's worldviews do tend to fall along similar philosophical lines. When seen from a ten-thousand-foot view, worldviews are really more similar than they are different along certain lines, whether epistemological or ontological. What results from this categorization is the emergence of many major philosophical worldviews present throughout history—nominalism, stoicism, skepticism, relativism, existentialism, agnosticism, determinism, to name just a few. To some extent, it is accurate to say that the seventeenth-century skepticism of René Descartes was a different expression of skepticism responding to a different cultural movement compared to the skepticism of the ancient Greeks. At the same time and despite their different expressions, it could be argued that the new skepticism is really just a revival of an old skepticism. As skepticism, these positions are both founded on the core epistemological principle that we cannot know some truths for certain. This argument is the same for other philosophical movements: nominalism, existentialism, and relativism are simply different threads of the same subjectivist cord. For that reason, Chesterton was able to claim that "new ideas are simply old mistakes" when surveying the rise and fall of many movements making a claim to novelty in every age.[6]

5. Chesterton, 41.

6. G.K. Chesterton, *Why I Am a Catholic*, in *The Collected Works of G.K. Chesterton* (San Francisco: Ignatius, 1990), 3:129.

Seen from this perspective, Chesterton's writings appear to have been consistently arguing against four major philosophical worldviews on freedom and meaning, ones that have been persistently present throughout history even to this day: determinism, existentialism, skepticism, and nihilism.

Determinism and skepticism are philosophies that Chesterton named and battled throughout his lifetime. With the flourishing of evolutionary theory in the late nineteenth century, many intellectuals and philosophers were adamant about reducing human life and actions to explanation by scientific laws and evolution. Dismayed by the reductionist dismissal of free will and divine purpose, Chesterton entered the intellectual arena to represent the Catholic Christian position that championed free will, a proper use of reason and science, and purpose behind the created world. From his early debates with Mr. Blatchford to his book *The Everlasting Man*, Chesterton's apologetical career is marked by a staunch defense of free will and the undeterminedness of life against both scientific and religious determinism.

Similar to determinism, the ideology of skepticism is one that Chesterton named and condemned for its debilitating effects on faith but most especially on reason. For modernity to demand logical or empirical proof for every act of the mind and will was, in Chesterton's opinion, absurd. He recognized that skepticism leads to paralysis of the will, thereby thwarting the intentional pursuit of a meaningful life. Perhaps it is not surprising that Chesterton's entire career is likewise marked by a battle against skepticism, as he was an apologist for Christianity among a modern intellectual class where skeptical tendencies were prevalent.

Moreover, existentialism was another target of Chesterton's argumentation, which he saw in his time in the form of neo-paganism, free love, individualism, and subjective morality. What united these subjectivist movements was a tendency to overemphasize free will, subjectivity, and personal creation of meaning.

Finally, nihilism, the position that existence has no ultimate meaning, was for Chesterton the most dangerous worldview and the most offensive to a world that struck him as anything but meaningless. In Chesterton's understanding, nihilism was essentially the destination of any imperfect worldview that did not correct its course.

THE SPECTRUM OF MEANING

These four worldviews are interrelated in a particular way that is relevant to this discussion—each of these worldviews, like Chesterton's worldview, takes a definitive stance on freedom and meaning. Where exactly they stand relative to each other and to Chesterton's worldview is best understood by placing them on a spectrum, which I will call the "spectrum of meaning" (Figure 4).

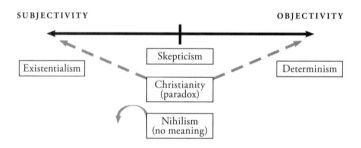

Figure 4. Spectrum of meaning.

The spectrum spans from the extreme of pure subjectivity to the other extreme of pure objectivity. First, at the extreme of pure subjectivity stands the philosophical position of existentialism, which makes the following claims about meaning and freedom: no meaning has been predetermined outside of the meaning that individuals have freely created for themselves, no one (not even God) can determine what is meaningful for one's life, there exists no objective standard for meaning or morality or truth, free will is the powerful capacity by which each person independently determines what is meaningful and moral and true for himself or herself, and any claim of objectivity is a result of social convention or societally agreed-upon standards. Of course, this short list does not encompass every single tenet of existentialism, but these are many of the core arguments and principles of people in this camp.

Second, at the other end of the spectrum, determinism occupies the position of pure objectivity with these claims: human freedom is ultimately an illusion due to an inability to alter a predetermined outcome, free will is powerless to create meaning outside of what has been objectively determined to be meaningful, and a subsequent state is pre-ordained by a preceding state. Of greatest interest to Chesterton were Calvinism, a form of spiritual determinism, and evolutionary determinism, a form of scientific determinism. For Calvinism, one's eternal spiritual fate is predetermined and unalterable by any act of the will. For evolutionary determinism, every so-called free action, thought, or feeling is a result of one's genetics and environment. Even love would be explained away as a product of natural selection, hormones locking into receptors, and neurons firing in select patterns.

Third, skepticism, asserting that no definitive claim can be made about the existence of meaning and freedom, occupies the middle of the spectrum, refusing to move confidently in the direction of objectivity or subjectivity. It wavers on every ultimate explanation of meaning and free will, asserting: we cannot claim for certain that meaning exists or that it is subjectively or objectively determined; we cannot claim for certain that we are free; and ultimately we cannot know for certain whether we exist, for this reality could be an illusion for all we know. The position of skepticism is one of ontological and epistemological incertitude, raising many questions about meaning and freedom but never providing ultimate answers.

Fourth, nihilism, the position that existence has no meaning, does not have a place on the spectrum insofar as it denies the existence of meaning. Objectively or subjectively determined meaning is of no proximate or ultimate significance. Because nihilism is a necessary outcome of any inadequate worldview that is misaligned with reality and does not correct itself, the other three worldviews on this spectrum—determinism, existentialism, and skepticism—can devolve into nihilism if they do not correct their principles on meaning and freedom. Any meaning that these worldviews once defended, whether objective or subjective, could ultimately become meaningless.

Fifth and finally, the question remains: Where does Chesterton's worldview stand on the spectrum of meaning, and which of these worldviews is most true to reality? One likely possibility for Chesterton's worldview is that it falls somewhere in the middle of the spectrum, given that Chesterton upholds and defends both the objective and subjective elements of life. In fact, he asserts as the core thesis of his work *Orthodoxy* that the Christian worldview is one that answers this "double spiritual need" for the "familiar and the unfamiliar": "I wish to set forth my faith as particularly answering this double spiritual need, the need for that mixture of the familiar and the unfamiliar which Christendom has rightly named romance."[7] Occupying the middle of the spectrum and claiming that life is to some extent objective and to some extent subjective would seem mostly aligned to Chesterton's worldview.

However, there exists another possibility, one that is even more characteristic of Chesterton's worldview and that may be considered the philosophical position on meaning and freedom that is most true to reality. That position on the spectrum is one

7. Chesterton, *Orthodoxy*, 2.

of "paradox," in Chesterton's understanding of paradox as both extremes operating at their full strength at the same time. Rather than a diluted mix of objectivity and subjectivity, like white and red mixed to become pink, perhaps Chesterton's worldview— that life is a story—holds that life is both very objective and very subjective at the same time, that subjectivity operates at its full strength within objectivity at its full strength, saying yes to both. Indeed, insofar as Chesterton's worldview is a Christian worldview through and through, this paradoxical position could also rightfully be understood to be the Christian philosophical position on freedom and meaning, for paradox is inherent to the dogmas of Christianity. Just as Jesus was not 50% God and 50% man but 100% God and 100% man in a way that we may not be able to fully comprehend, could this not also be the Christian logic for answering the ancient ontological question of to what extent meaning is determined and undetermined? And would it not be an intuitive conclusion that the meaning of life is both 100% determined and 100% undetermined, that we are very free to determine meaning within God's created order but that God has determined the bounds of what could be meaningful, set the objective standard for truth and goodness, and already determined the "best" goal that we could take any number of paths to? This would seem to be a logical outcome if there exists an all-powerful divine will that coexists with and somehow does not conflict with a powerful human will, both of which are simultaneously ordering creation in a meaningful way. This would also be a logical outcome considering another fact, that God has already established an objective standard for truth and goodness but that each of us has our own unique subjective path toward the objective good (although arriving at the objective is not predetermined to happen). Finally, this would be a logical outcome of a third fact about divine and human freedom, whereby God is able to create meaning in two ways—from nothing, and by ordering what has been created—while we can only create in one way—by ordering what has been created. Even if the coexistence of 100% and 100% makes less rational sense than that of 50% and 50% making up a whole, our limited ability to understand would not in itself be sufficient grounds for disproving this truth.

PARADOX

Resting the main weight of this argument on one key paradox is a move that is appropriate and defensible in a reading of Chesterton, the prince of paradox. While he is often accused of intellectual cowardice or laziness for falling back on paradoxes, Chesterton points out that the use of paradox is nearly inevitable in philosophy: "If [Mr. McCabe] asks me why I introduce what he calls paradoxes into a philosophical problem, I answer, because all philosophical problems tend to become paradoxical."[8] Not only does philosophy tend toward paradox, but so does religion: "Every genuine religion that ever existed on earth as distinct from a mere philosophy has been marked by two main peculiarities. The first is a great trend towards practicality; the second is a great trend towards paradox."[9] For an example, he points to the Beatitudes and many other of Christ's strikingly paradoxical statements, suggesting that paradox is a mechanism of expressing the complexity of truths in a perceivable way.

These scriptural examples and other paradoxes in Christianity are evidence that paradox is inherent to Christianity. In fact, paradox lies at the heart of Christian dogmas. As Chesterton pointed out, God is both three and one at the same time in a way we may not be able to fully wrap our minds around, but our limited capacity to understand does not detract from the inherent truth.[10] Likewise, Jesus was not 50% God and 50% man like a demigod, but rather 100% God and 100% man at the same

8. Chesterton, *Heretics*, 166.

9. G.K. Chesterton, "On Short Cuts," *Daily News*, March 11, 1905, cutting, no. 148 in Printed Ephemera I, GKC Library.

10. See Chesterton, *Heretics*, 86–87.

time.[11] Far from being a petty nuance for theologians to argue over, this makes all the difference for the Christian faith. For if Jesus were any less than fully God, then he could not save us, but if he were any less than fully human, then humanity, in Christ, could not have offered the sufficient expiating sacrifice that it needed to offer. As a third example, the Bible is not a human book with some divine influence, nor a divine dictation that man recorded, but a revelatory collection fully authored by God and fully authored by man at the same time.

Thus, Chesterton's employment of paradox was an expression not of the absence but of the presence of his thinking, and perhaps he, more than other intellectuals of his time, was able to perceive the deeper truths that coexisting extremes revealed.

PENDULUM

Upon grouping the countless philosophical movements throughout history along ontological and epistemological lines and identifying any trends regarding their emphases on objectivity and subjectivity, a very peculiar observation emerges—that every few decades, society has a tendency to move from one extreme of the spectrum to the other, precisely as a "reaction" to the inadequacies of the opposite extreme. In other words, if society is said to be overemphasizing subjectivity today, that could be readily explained as a reaction to a societal overemphasis of objectivity decades before, but once society recognizes that extreme subjectivity is a failure, it will likely react by over-stressing objectivity. To take a few concrete examples of how this has shown itself in Western culture, there have been many excessively objective movements of the political, cultural, and religious kinds. Authoritarianism is a form of political objectivity that suppresses personal freedom and expression, often arising out of a societal demand for unified order and rule. Calvinism is a form of

11. Chesterton, *Everlasting Man*, 271–273.

religious determinism that negates the role of human freedom in altering one's eternal state, arising during the Reformation in reaction to the Catholic belief that humans can gain merit through righteous action on earth.

On the flipside, societal over-emphases of subjectivity have appeared time and again throughout history, often as a reaction to the oppressiveness of overly objective movements. The philosophical movement of "existentialism," especially the existentialism proposed by French thinker Jean-Paul Sartre in the twentieth century, was a postmodern reaction to World Wars I and II, whose unbounded destruction of human civilizations, discarding of millions of human lives, and sadistic manipulation of science cast doubt on the philosophical assumptions up to that point in history. Existentialism flipped the script from the ages-old philosophical truism "essence precedes existence," which defended that each person's essence is objectively determined even before he or she exists. Instead, building off the Nietzschean will to power, Sartre famously claimed that "existence precedes essence," whereby people first come into existence and thereafter define who they are and what is meaningful for them alone through the act of the will. This postmodern over-emphasis of subjectivity in the form of existentialism is perhaps the dominant undercurrent of our society today.

This observation of short-lived reactionary movements, fashions, and moods was one that Chesterton made in his book *Where All Roads Lead.* When considering the Catholic Church in its relation to the countless new philosophies, trends, fads, and movements arising in each generation, it became very clear to Chesterton that Catholicism was not a reactionary "movement" or a "mood" like every other movement he observed, but instead a divinely sourced, eternal system that outlasted every short-lived mood that opposed it: "If the proper duration of a movement is twenty years, what sort of movement is it that lasts nearly two thousand? If a fashion should last no longer than Impressionism, what sort of fashion is it that lasts about fifty times as long? Is it just barely conceivable that it is not a fashion?"[12]

While the pendulum swings from one philosophical extreme to the next throughout history, reacting to the immediately preceding mistaken movement only to repeat an even earlier mistake, could it not be that the two-thousand-year-old Christian philosophy has endured precisely because it has been the most right and most true to reality, not emphasizing one extreme over the other but upholding the tenuous balance of both extremes at the same time? To honor both objectivity and subjectivity at their full strength at the same time—that is the genius solution offered by the Christian philosophy. If any other philosophical movement has even attempted to occupy this paradoxical position, Chesterton might have us believe that only Catholic Christianity would be successful in doing so. For not only is the Christian God's nature a paradox—in the sense of the Trinity being three and one at the same time—but Catholic Christianity was the only system in Chesterton's experience to have been consistently "catholic," in the sense of "universal," capaciously holding all truths (even seemingly conflicting truths) in cohesive unity, where all peoples, all ideas, and all philosophical principles could find their home in this one trysting place: "But the Church is not a movement but a meeting-place; the trysting-place of all the truths in the world."[13]

TWO MARKS OF A HEALTHY PHILOSOPHY— UNIVERSALITY AND LIFE

Before considering in detail each of the four major philosophical positions and their tenets on meaning and freedom, we might first consider two "marks" or practical tests that help answer the central question "What worldview is most true to reality?"

12. G.K. Chesterton, *Where All Roads Lead*, in *The Collected Works*, 3:30.
13. Chesterton, *Why I Am a Catholic*, 132.

Oftentimes, a practical test is more useful than an abstract theorization in determining the inherent truth of a claim, and this approach would certainly be wise to apply to an entire system of claims. A philosophical argument may please the ear and strike the listener as sound only for the listener to find that the argument lends no practical value. On a larger scale, a philosophical system of claims like atheistic materialism or Sartrean existentialism may strike many people as plausible explanations of reality, but from a practical standpoint, these systems tend to have an effect of shutting doors and leading to dead ends rather than clearing the road ahead or cracking the code of reality. Even if you buy the argument of the atheist, the only real reply you can muster is an acquiescent "Oh," as Chesterton pointed out.[14] If God exists, then everything has a story tied to it and the adventure has only begun, but if God does not exist, well, none of this ultimately means anything.

This leads to the first of two marks of a worldview most true to reality that Chesterton noted: universality of application. If a worldview were most true to reality, we would expect that worldview to explain and pertain to every detail of life. Something in us demands such a universal worldview that explains every thing, every place, every time, every field of knowledge, and every material and immaterial phenomenon. It would be no good for a worldview to be pertinent to only one generation, or to apply to the future and not the past or to the past and not the future. Nor would it be satisfactory if a philosophical worldview (if it is most true to reality) applied to only one culture or people but not to the rest of humanity. If a certain people possessed a worldview most true to reality, they would either hide the arcane knowledge from the rest of the world out of self-concern or be itching to share the key to unlock reality that all people for all time have been searching for on their ontological quest.

14. Chesterton, *Where All Roads Lead*, 38.

It struck Chesterton as no coincidence, then, that Catholicism was the "universal philosophy," not only claiming to be "catholic" (meaning "universal") but also proving through practical tests to be universally true. For Chesterton, all roads did lead to Rome. The rich and the poor, the Jew and the Greek, the brown and black and white, the academic and the uneducated, the celibate priest and the parent—all extreme human experiences and every person in between could find their home within the bounds of Catholicism's capaciousness. While most other narratives of the world preached that prosperity comes to those who climb the ladder of achievement and material gain, Christianity claimed that prosperity and blessedness come to those who lower themselves. Not everyone can move up, but everyone can move down. The philosophy at the top applies only to those who make it to the top in their lifetime, while the philosophy at the bottom is the philosophy of the masses, and each person has the choice of meeting Christ where he appeared—at the bottom, where all might be gathered.

What is striking, however, is that universality is not in itself a failsafe test of a worldview most true to reality because, as Chesterton observed, "there is such a thing as a narrow universality; there is such a thing as a small and cramped eternity."[15] Chesterton noticed this narrow universality most prominently in the materialism of his day, which claimed to explain all of material existence in a final way yet giving "the sense of it covering everything and the sense of it leaving everything out."[16] The materialistic philosophy seeks to explain everything—even spiritual experiences and that which cannot be empirically proven, like love—by way of appeal to material phenomena. The same narrow universality is recognizable in a scientific determinism grounded in evolutionary theory. Evolutionary theory is not a

15. Chesterton, *Orthodoxy*, 13.
16. Chesterton, 16.

harmful scientific theory, and as a science, it does not conflict with a Christian view of creation. But as a philosophical position, "evolutionism" will go so far as to try to explain everything by way of two causes, genetics and the environment. Why did that man fall in love with that woman? Because he was genetically disposed to be attracted to her due to natural selection, and the environment he grew up in conditioned him to like that sort of woman, the evolutionary determinist would say. Nothing in this explanation is erroneous or anti-Christian, but when the evolutionary determinist loses sight of the other factors beyond genetics and environment at play, his once-plausible explanation devolves into a logical monomania.

Related to the first test of universality is the second test—that a worldview is like life. For Chesterton, a narrow universality, in spite of its universality, goes hand-in-hand with a lifeless worldview. It was these very monomaniacs who were fixed on one all-explaining theory—whether materialism or evolutionary determinism or the power of the will to define all truth—whose heads Chesterton wished to break open to give oxygen and light—that is, life. The people of one mad idea were tolerable to be around in spite of, not because of, their all-explaining philosophy.

Another way to think about whether a worldview is bringing about life is to look at the behavior and demeanor that it produces. Where there is joy, peace, goodness, common sense, productivity, healthy relationships, and concern for others, that worldview is likely to be life-giving. On the other hand, if there is pusillanimity, isolation, fearful self-defense, and outward bitterness, that worldview is likely drying up life.

Another consideration for identifying a worldview that is life-like is to look out at the masses of humanity to observe how they approach life. While majority representation does not directly translate to what is most true, nevertheless, the masses are the ones going about life most authentically, as Chesterton would have us see. The masses are the ones convinced that something is wrong with humanity, that life has a purpose, and that God is the benevolent Author of the story of creation despite the hardships of life. In contrast to this majority view, the dominant philosophical systems are almost without exception the product of armchair philosophers whose personal lives are woeful in many cases. Even if people try to attribute the insanity of Nietzsche to influences outside of his worldview, they cannot defend that this figure was happy. In many cases, the determinism, skepticism, existentialism, or nihilism of these philosophers arose out of a personal rebellion to the experiences of life. These philosophical systems of thought may have been authentic responses to personal experiences of life, but in responding to life, they give the sense of getting farther from explaining life and paving a practical path forward. To be told "everything is predetermined" is a quick way to lose all motivation, and to be told the opposite—"go be whatever you want"—provides no practical direction to go.

As Chesterton knew deeply, the Catholic philosophy was the universal philosophy that was like life, and it alone was able to achieve this because of its ability to hold up all values in paradoxical tension. It is a philosophy that can uphold the ideal destination of humanity while honoring each unique path of getting there. It is a philosophy accessible to the uneducated and the intellectual alike. It is a philosophy that sheds light on every detail of life, from the microscopic cells of multicellular organisms to the deep physics of the ever-expanding cosmos. It is a philosophy that provides an answer for the past, a guide for the present, and a promise that it will answer every unanticipated situation and dilemma of the future, for it is universal and true to reality. It is one of many philosophies and one of many stories, yet it is universal like no other philosophy and meaningful like no other story. The discoverers of this philosophy, when they find it, will find the worldview that is most true to reality: "It is a story and in that sense one of a hundred stories; only it is a true story. It is a philosophy and in that sense one of a hundred philosophies; only it is a philosophy that is like life."[17]

17. Chesterton, *Everlasting Man*, 408–409.

CHAPTER **8**

Determinism

Pure Objectivity

"Now it is the charge against the main deductions of the materialist that, right or wrong, they gradually destroy his humanity; I do not mean only kindness, I mean hope, courage, poetry, initiative, all that is human. For instance, when materialism leads men to complete fatalism (as it generally does), it is quite idle to pretend that it is in any sense a liberating force. . . . They may well call their law the 'chain' of causation. It is the worst chain that ever fettered a human being."[1]

DETERMINISM

Strains of determinism, existentialism, and skepticism are all running through our postmodern culture, just as they did during Chesterton's time in early-twentieth-century London. And while our culture is far from a framework of pure objectivity, nevertheless, deterministic strains are still apparent under both materialist and spiritualist forms. Chesterton came of age shortly after the discoveries of Charles Darwin, whose evolutionary theory shook the scientific and religious spheres with its novel assumptions about who a human being was and how the human species originated. To the secularly minded, Darwin's evolutionary theory was enough to unravel the entire project of Christianity,

1. G.K. Chesterton, *Orthodoxy* (Park Ridge, IL: Word on Fire Classics, 2017), 18–19.

whose revelatory texts told of God creating the world in seven days. If interpreting the book of Genesis literally—in the sense that God did indeed create the world in seven earth days—of course evolutionary theory conflicted with Christianity. The Catholic tradition does not take this purely literal interpretation of Genesis and therefore does not view evolutionary theory as conflicting with Genesis, but it makes sense why many scientific minds during the late nineteenth and early twentieth centuries were quick to shake off the millennia-old assumptions about divine purpose and design in favor of an exciting new theory.

In lieu of the assumptions of divine objectivity and order, a new objective framework took its place. For many scientific minds buying into evolutionary theory as an all-explaining worldview, all actions of living organisms (including so-called free and rational human beings) could be explained by two forces: genetics and the environment. Why did that person rob the bank? Because his prehistoric ancestors may have learned to steal from neighboring tribes to survive, and perhaps he was raised in such a way that he saw the act as logical, the scientifically minded may argue. Why did that woman fall in love with that man? Because her female ancestors tended to be attracted to men with those features, and prehistorically such features were typical of more "fit" men likely to survive and pass on their genes, and the culture may have influenced her romantic preferences, the evolutionary biologist may say. Every human decision, from weeding the garden to burying the dead, becomes the object of the double-lensed hermeneutic of the evolutionary biologist. And for Chesterton, while these tests have some basis for understanding influences on human action, they have the effect of stripping every decision of purpose.

If a certain kind of evolutionary biologist can be said to make deterministic claims about human decisions, a certain kind of physicist can be said to do the same. In a materialist view, a complex pattern of neuron firings creates even those phenomena that were formerly understood to be metaphysical, such as falling in love, performing an act of justice, or offering up a prayer to the divine. Moreover, in the minds of some physicists, those phenomena are not subject to human decision but are predetermined by a chain of physical causes. The result is not only the reduction of immaterial realities to material ones, but also the elimination of human free will. While the work of physics does not conflict with a properly constituted Christian framework, and in fact provides very helpful new ways of understanding the material world, the effect when attempting to explain all material and immaterial phenomena without exception is anything but liberating. This chain of causation proposed by these scientific materialists truly was a chain of slavery in Chesterton's mind.

One other form of determinism that Chesterton argued against was spiritual determinism. Whether seen as a divine being or a mystical force, spiritual determinism believes in some force (a god, karma, or fate) as predestining a future state of affairs. It may take the form of the guaranteed retributive justice of karma—if you cheat someone, karma will ensure that you will pay the price in the future to restore justice, even if no one ever knew of the original act. It could take the form of fate— that woman was fated to meet her future husband in a certain restaurant after her car broke down in a snowstorm. It also has appeared in religious forms—the belief that "all people go to heaven" is a thoroughly deterministic claim. No matter how bad one's actions may be, God's love is believed to be so powerful as to overcome any and all remnants of evil. As comforting as this belief may be, it leaves us wondering whether an evil person is free to face the consequences of his actions, perhaps even consequences he willfully chose to face. Similarly, it would destroy the basis of risk if you could never lose money that you gambled, observed Chesterton: "It would not be worthwhile to bet if a bet were not binding. . . . If I vow to be faithful I must be cursed when I am unfaithful, or there is no fun in vowing."[2] It was all of these forms of material and spiritual determinism that Chesterton had in mind when arguing against determinism, a pure objectivity that destroys the drama of life by drying up the wellspring of subjectivity.

TENETS OF DETERMINISM

Whether material or spiritual determinism, what unites all forms of determinism is the notion of necessity—that a particular outcome is preordained by former conditions. From a more scientific perspective, necessity is the result of scientific laws that govern all physical processes and forces. In this view, everything from a sunrise to animal behavior is bound to happen due to the laws that govern matter down to the level of atoms and molecules making up the material world. Even if a future state is unpredictable by our knowledge, such as how a pet dog will act tomorrow, scientific determinism would claim that today's internal and external conditions (stimuli and chemicals, for example) will preordain the dog's behavior.

Applying determinism to evolutionary theory, many evolutionary biologists make the argument that the evolution of humans from more primitive lifeforms was destined to happen. Usually it is the same scientists who argue for a repeatable history of life, claiming that evolutionary history is both orthogenetic and progressive. Two principles are apparent from these scientific arguments: life could not have been another way, and life is trending toward a higher, more complex form by an automatic process. The "automatic" process is conditioned by natural selection, they might argue. We will see shortly how problems arise when science is erroneously treated as a philosophical worldview.

Regarding spiritual determinism, to incorporate necessity into religion might look like downplaying the role of free will,

---

2. Chesterton, 123.

attributing one's spiritual state to fate or to God's inviolable sovereignty. Some Eastern philosophies contain deterministic threads, treating fate as a force governing the world. Within Christianity, determinism has shown itself in Calvinism, which holds that souls are predestined by God to either heaven or hell. Whether with scientific or religious determinism, necessity and free will tend to be inversely proportional.

PROBLEMS WITH DETERMINISM
Science Oversteps Its Bounds

Why is science relevant to this discussion of philosophical worldviews? Science as a field of study has the task of explaining *how* physical processes occur. However, problems arise when science leaves its realm of physical explanations and invades the realm of philosophy, the science of asking *why*. Science is often erroneously confounded with scientism, which is a philosophical position on the role of science in explaining reality as a whole. When science and philosophy enter each other's fields, errant worldviews—like scientism and determinism—can arise. To offer an example, scientism can easily produce this deterministic philosophical argument through extrapolation on one evolutionary theory: "If certain biological states are preordained by current conditions, then any future state (spiritual, mental, psychological, social) is similarly preordained and necessary, given current conditions." Applying Chesterton's critique, a scientific explanation is erroneously treated as "all-explaining," except science *qua* science is not meant to be all-explaining. No wonder scientism, determinism, and materialism are too simplistic to explain this existence—one scientific theory is stretched to fit the world. Science and philosophy work best through dialogue that recognizes the domain of the other, wherein each honors and learns from the authority of the other.

Denial of Free Will

As one might guess, many problems arise when the role of free will is diminished or denied. In scientific determinism, the element of free choice is undermined as soon as one's decisions are fully explained by scientific laws, genetics, and the environment. Choices are not really free because one's genetics and environment have disposed him toward making them. All of one's actions are "a chain of causation," not a series of freely made decisions but inevitable outcomes.[3] Taken all the way to its effects on everyday life, this determinism "gradually destroy[s] [one's] humanity; . . . hope, courage, poetry, initiative, all that is human."[4] Life is robbed of adventure if one is forced to be kind, to be hopeful, to be courageous, to be creative and poetic, and to be driven. One's life would not be much of a story if it had to end a certain way. As discussed earlier, what makes life an adventurous story is that it might end in any way based on how we freely make decisions about the unknown future.

Denial of Responsibility

A particular aspect of humanity that is lost with determinism is responsibility, a key contributing factor to the thrill of the moral life. In his autobiography, Chesterton recounts, "It was the Determinist who said that I could not be responsible at all . . . shouting that no man ought to be blamed for anything he did, because it was all hereditary and environment."[5] Responsibility is a gift from the divine Author that enables his human characters to take ownership over the story's details and direction of the plot. The moral life becomes exciting when it is perceived as a series of freely made decisions that affect the story of oneself

3. Chesterton, 18.

4. Chesterton, 18.

5. G.K. Chesterton, *The Autobiography of G.K. Chesterton*, in *The Collected Works of G.K. Chesterton* (San Francisco: Ignatius, 1988), 16:173–174.

and of others, for better or for worse. If free choice is denied through deterministic theory, the end result is "stark paralysis, touching the practical conduct of human life."[6]

One such strain of determinism that discourages responsibility is the assumption that humanity is improving by an automatic process. As Chesterton rightly puts it, "If we are bound to improve, we need not trouble to improve. The pure doctrine of progress is the best of all reasons for not being a progressive."[7] If our story is bound to end happily, then our decisions have no effect on the ending of the story.

Speaking now to religious determinism, the emphasis is often the complete sovereignty of God at the expense of human freedom. This might look like God's forcing one to receive grace or even compelling one to do evil. It might take the form of double predestination as found in Calvinism—God elects some souls to heaven and condemns the others to hell, a sovereign act of the divine will in which human actions have no effect in determining the outcome. Quoted earlier, this passage sums up the drama of life that results from having responsibility over one's actions:

> To the Catholic every other daily act is dramatic dedication to the service of good or of evil. To the Calvinist no act can have that sort of solemnity, because the person doing it has been dedicated from eternity, and is merely filling up his time until the crack of doom. . . . The difference is that to a Christian of my kind this short earthly life is intensely thrilling and precious; to a Calvinist like Mr. Shaw it is confessedly automatic and uninteresting. To me these threescore years

---

6. G.K. Chesterton, *The Well and the Shallows*, in *The Collected Works of G.K. Chesterton* (San Francisco: Ignatius, 1990), 3:393.

7. Chesterton, *Orthodoxy*, 110.

and ten are the battle. . . . To me earthly life is the drama; to him it is the epilogue.[8]

Denial of Design and Purpose

Another result of physical determinism is the denial of design, which can then lead to a denial of any purpose in creation. To claim that "everything is as it must always have been, being unfolded without fault from the beginning" is to open oneself to the denial of design, because the inviolability of the created order is usually attributed to impersonal laws of nature rather than a willful divine choice.[9] While for Chesterton every detail of the created world strongly suggests an element of divine choice, determinism can undermine this element of choice. For instance, the determinist may claim that "the leaf on the tree is green because it could never have been anything else."[10] If colors of nature do not have an element of intentional detail, then other created things may not either. Soon the whole created order appears to be an accident, in the sense of a mechanical sequence void of intention. Dread "creep[s] like a slow paralysis" over those who see no purpose in the created world: "When first it was even hinted that the universe may not be a great design, . . . when there is no longer even a vague idea of purposes or presences, then the many-coloured forest really is a rag-bag and all the pageant of the dust only a dustbin."[11]

8. G.K. Chesterton, *What's Wrong with the World*, in *The Collected Works of G.K. Chesterton* (San Francisco: Ignatius, 1987), 4:153–154.

9. Chesterton, *Orthodoxy*, 55.

10. Chesterton, 55.

11. Chesterton, *Autobiography*, 326.

THE RESPONSE OF CHRISTIANITY TO DETERMINISM

Admits Settledness

The response of the Christian worldview to determinism is to admit to determinedness but not at the expense of un-determinedness. We recall that the Catholic Church is the advocate of both objectivity and subjectivity. Applying the spectrum of meaning presented earlier, the Church says "yes" to both extremes on the spectrum. The balance is sensitive, and errant philosophies tend to take one extreme truth too far. Chesterton calls this a "heresy," and the Church responds by reasserting both sides, holding both extremes in paradoxical tension.[12]

Although determinedness looks different within the Christian worldview and the deterministic worldview, these two worldviews can agree on the principle of determinedness in this world. For the Christian worldview, determinedness manifests itself in design, divine purpose, and objective morality. For the deterministic worldview, it may show itself as fate, predestination, or automatic unfolding. Christianity admits to the idea of settledness but attempts to explain it in a more capacious, balanced, and practical way. Because this worldview is able to make room for both settledness and unsettledness, "the Christian is quite free to believe that there is a considerable amount of settled order and inevitable development in the universe." This is unlike the determinist, whose cramped system of one idea cannot admit any trace of unsettledness: "But the materialist is not allowed to admit into his spotless machine the slightest speck of spiritualism or miracle."[13] The irony of materialism presents itself in the previous quote—this so-called "all-explaining" worldview cannot explain transcendental phenomena according to its physical principles, which in fact are not meant to explain the spiritual

---

12. G.K. Chesterton, *The Thing: Why I Am a Catholic*, in *The Collected Works*, 3:317.

13. Chesterton, *Orthodoxy*, 18.

realm anyway. To save the determinist from the "slow paralysis" of impracticality and the "nightmare" of destiny arising from the denial of purpose in the smallest to the largest created things, he is invited to awake to this world and don the lenses of purpose so that he may see things as they are.[14]

Against the determinist's claim that the past preordains and prejudices the present and the future, the voice of Christianity admits that "as a fact it is impossible for anybody to avoid using the past."[15] While the determinist treats the past as a problematic influence on the future, Christianity rejoices that the past bears relevance on the present and the future. The continuity of past, present, and future allows life to be a romance with "irrevocable result[s]."[16] God takes our actions and their consequences seriously. As Author, he does not erase details of the past or skip around the story. His power is even more evident in his ability to write with our successes and mistakes, which do leave marks on his story. It is no surprise that the integrity of this position is cultivated in the garden of the Catholic Church, which Chesterton describes as "a thing of the future and the present, as well as the past."[17]

Affirms Unsettledness

Having agreed to the principle of settledness in this world, Christianity then invites the determinist to admit unsettledness into his system, so that he may embody his unique role as a character of a grand romance story. Christianity first resists the deterministic principle of automatic improvement as applied to human activity. While a strong scientific case can be made for automatic improvement in evolution (though many evolutionary biologists question this view), it does not follow that automatic

14. Chesterton, *Autobiography*, 326.
15. Chesterton, *The Well and the Shallows*, 422.
16. Chesterton, *Orthodoxy*, 123.
17. Chesterton, *The Well and the Shallows*, 422.

improvement occurs in politics, economics, and spirituality. A white post does not become whiter or remain white by an automatic process.[18] Just so, governments, economies, and especially the human heart, if left to themselves, will "naturally tend to grow worse."[19] What improvement requires is vigilance over laziness and activity over passivity. The final destination may be settled; in fact, Chesterton asserts the need for a clear vision of the end goal.[20] But the process toward this settled goal is not automatic. A creative power and an effective force are necessary to efficaciously alter the present toward the future goal. Christianity calls this creative and efficacious power "free will."

Chesterton makes a helpful distinction between evolution, progress, and reform, clarifying the need for free will. According to Chesterton, evolution is an "automatic unrolling."[21] He finds no problem admitting that some processes, like the evolution of species, are automatic processes that may not require free will. He even allows for the entertainment of the idea that evolution tends toward improvement. But if automatic improvement is a natural process, "it must be fairly simple. The world might conceivably be working towards one consummation, but hardly towards any particular arrangement of many qualities."[22] This is where the Christian worldview diverges from automatic processes. Because automatic improvement cannot lead to anything better than simple culmination, an objectively determined purpose cannot be reached by a passive process, as it is anything but simple. It is a key of complex shape, fitting one precise keyhole.[23] It is a romance story of a finite creature fitting into an overarching

18. Chesterton, *Orthodoxy*, 114–115.

19. Chesterton, 114.

20. Chesterton, 105.

21. Chesterton, 105.

22. Chesterton, 110.

23. G.K. Chesterton, *The Everlasting Man*, in *The Everlasting Man: A Guide to G.K. Chesterton's Masterpiece*, ed. Dale Ahlquist (Elk Grove Village, IL: Word on Fire, 2023), 356–358.

story fashioned by an infinite being. It is the "trysting-place" of paradoxical but consistent truths, accounting for objectivity and subjectivity, determinedness and un-determinedness, the familiar and the unfamiliar.[24] It is a goal reached not by the passive process of evolution nor by blind progress not knowing its end goal. Instead, it is a complex shape conformed to by reform: "[Reform] means that we see a certain thing out of shape and we mean to put it into shape. And we know what shape."[25] By the active process of free will and the clear vision of the settled goal, we set out to re-form our lives against the natural tendency of this world to de-form our lives.

Though the deterministic claim that this life story is bound to end happily ("happily ever after") may seem better than the possibility of having sad endings, this life story would fail to be romantic and would hardly satisfy as a story if it could only end one way, even if that one ending were happy. This deterministic thread appears more often than we might imagine within various Christian denominations. It can take the explicit form of double predestination, the belief that God has already determined where every soul is going after death—heaven or hell. However, it often appears in less obvious forms, and its implications are toxic to Christianity and to the view of life as a story. It is the flatness of determinism disguised as Christian hope when we hear a Christian, often well-meaning, exclaim that all people are going to heaven. The Church exists for the sake of proclaiming and achieving that happy ending for all souls, but in expressing hope, it nevertheless admits the "darkness of that potential tragedy" that some souls could freely choose eternal isolation.[26]

The Christian worldview is a war cry to save the romantic and story-like qualities from the threats of determinism. Because

24. G.K. Chesterton, *Why I Am a Catholic*, in *The Collected Works*, 3:132.
25. Chesterton, *Orthodoxy*, 105.
26. Chesterton, *The Thing*, 150.

an enemy exists who is constantly de-forming our story, we must embrace the battle against evil in order to fight for the good that we love, knowing that the good will not be achieved by an automatic process. The potential for danger and ruin charges our every action with thrill and adventure, since every moral action efficaciously re-forms or de-forms our story. Because the limited materials of this life are the very sacraments that reveal the design of God and are the very means by which to carry out the divine Author's story, savvy use of creation is required to see God's purpose charging all things. Because the story may end in any way, individuals may participate freely in the story so that God might bring about the best ending, which will only come about through free participation. When the storybook is revealed at the end of time, the characters will witness the complex, romantic narrative that was written through the effort of their free participation. Knowing that it was "the hardest obligation and the steepest adventure" to arrive at that utopia, those souls will give thanks to God for taking their actions and desires seriously, and they will humbly concede that they would not have wanted it any other way.[27]

27. Chesterton, *Orthodoxy*, 123.

CHAPTER 9

Existentialism

Pure Subjectivity

"Mr. Bernard Shaw has put the view in a perfect epigram: 'The golden rule is that there is no golden rule.' We are more and more to discuss details in art, politics, literature. A man's opinion on tramcars matters; his opinion on Botticelli matters; his opinion on all things does not matter. He may turn over and explore a million objects, but he must not find that strange object, the universe; for if he does he will have a religion, and be lost. Everything matters— except everything."[1]

EXISTENTIALISM

"No one can tell me what to do with my life." "My body, my choice." "Invent yourself." These are only some of the familiar rally cries of a pure subjectivism pervading the political and social spheres of the twenty-first century. Political conversations are often dominated by a belligerent appeal to rights, and cultural movements are centered around individuality; it has the appearance that each person's identity must be guarded against the oppressive social constructs created by those in power. The binary designation of "male and female" is too clean of a categorization and too socially constructed for the subjectivist. For the subjectivist, the fact that societies up to now have upheld

---

1. G.K. Chesterton, *Heretics*, in *The Collected Works of G.K. Chesterton* (San Francisco: Ignatius, 1986), 1:40.

marriage as between a man and a woman is most likely due to the people in power saying it is so rather than it being an inherent truth about reality. The same goes for many other assumptions and truths taken for granted. Every truth is up for redefining, since the validity of truth is grounded in the subjective experience of each person and how true a truth is for that person.

We may be tempted to think that these societal undercurrents are unique to the twenty-first century, and in some ways their expressions are indeed particular to the historical events of our current age. However, it is easy to identify throughout Chesterton's writings that a pure subjectivism was prevalent in his time, and the examples are many. "The golden rule is that there is no golden rule," "the spirit of license," "free lust," and "the mood" are all expressions of a subjectivism that Chesterton noticed in the culture of his day. Chesterton also noticed a generational shift toward an obsessive defense of personal rights without asking more foundational questions about where those rights came from and why humans should have rights at all: "A whole generation has been taught to talk nonsense at the top of its voice about having 'a right to life' and 'a right to experience' and 'a right to happiness.'"[2] Chesterton was quite familiar with the argument that "actions are only wrong if they are bad for society," a defense for subjective morality that is as impractical and illogical as it is prevalent.[3] In Chesterton's day and most especially today, freedom, individuality, and personal rights are treated as the highest values. These defenses of subjective expression against the perceived oppression of objectivity may come from a good place and can be traced to the noble values of God-given identity, individuality, freedom, and rights. The issue, however, as Chesterton would have us believe, is that the

2. G.K. Chesterton, *The Autobiography of G.K. Chesterton*, in *The Collected Works of G.K. Chesterton* (San Francisco: Ignatius, 1988), 16:324–325.

3. G.K. Chesterton, *Why I Am a Catholic*, in *The Collected Works of G.K. Chesterton* (San Francisco: Ignatius, 1990), 3:130.

subjective values are taken to an extreme, treated as inviolable, and defended against other equally important values of justice and obedience to a moral order. To take one value and pit it against the others is how Chesterton defines heresy, and it is no wonder that the "heresy" of subjectivism naturally devolves into a cramped egoism that hardly resembles the Christian faith, which upholds and defends each person's unique individuality and subjective experience of the world within the bounds of an ordering objectivity.

Interestingly, before the term was conceived in the mid-twentieth century, Chesterton keenly perceived a postmodern form of subjectivism that has arguably been the dominant philosophical undercurrent of the past century—existentialism. Existentialism is a philosophical position that holds that people define their individuality, identity, meaning, and truths through acts of the will. The famous aphorism of existentialism, coined by the existentialist philosopher Jean-Paul Sartre (1905–1980), is that "existence precedes essence," which, as we will see, is a stark denial of objectivism. But before Sartre rose to the scene in the mid-twentieth century, Chesterton already was arguing against this stream of consciousness before it was even called existentialism: "If we want to uproot inherent cruelties or lift up lost populations we cannot do it with the scientific theory that matter precedes mind; we can do it with the supernatural theory that mind precedes matter."[4] Many modern-day historians have traced existentialism back to Søren Kierkegaard (1813–1855) and Friedrich Nietzsche (1844–1900), who both defended subjective experience despite their differing positions. While Chesterton never lived to combat Sartre's existentialism directly, he had the benefit of living after Nietzsche, whose nihilistic existentialism he vehemently combated and traced to the extreme subjectivism

4. G.K. Chesterton, *Orthodoxy* (Park Ridge, IL: Word on Fire Classics, 2017), 143.

of his time. The way that Chesterton wrote about Nietzsche is close to how he would treat the Sartrean existentialism of our day. As we will see, ontological pluripotency, as in the form of "accepting [all paths] like Nietzsche," is a clear mark of existentialism, which holds that you can become anything you want, which ironically causes people to get stuck at the crossroads because of all the choices and possibilities with no indication of what paths are better than others.[5]

And as we shall also see in all of these flawed philosophies, even while some of these existentialist philosophers tried to defend their philosophical position from becoming a nihilistic existentialism, the tenets of existentialism clearly point to and logically result in nihilism. If all meaning is individually defined, even if that can be called meaningful, the subjective experience comes to a quick end in death, and no meaning endures. Chesterton felt like he was watching the inevitable crash of these philosophies from a ten-thousand-foot view when he took their claims and followed them to their conclusions: "I can see the inevitable smash of the philosophies of Schopenhauer and Tolstoy, Nietzsche and Shaw, as clearly as an inevitable railway smash could be seen from a balloon. They are all on the road to the emptiness of the asylum. For madness may be defined as using mental activity so as to reach mental helplessness; and they have nearly reached it."[6]

TENETS OF EXISTENTIALISM
Freedom

Although existentialism may take on many forms and mean different things to different philosophers, *existentialism* will be used here as a general term to represent many of the core principles usually attributed to this philosophical position. The first

5. Chesterton, 39.
6. Chesterton, 39.

tenet is emphasis on personal freedom. Existentialist freedom, in practice, often looks like absence of restraint, the power of choice, and the capacity to create values and meaning to one's liking. Because life is about making of it what you desire, you must be "free" from external and internal restraints and expectations, which inherently limit the plan you are carrying out. This absence of restraint is related to power of choice, which holds that one is more "free" to become anything he desires when more choices are available. These forms of freedom operate under the assumption that no objective meaning and values—truth, goodness, beauty, justice—exist; no meaning exists externally to be found, and no standard exists to determine what is true, what is good, and what is beautiful. We will soon see how these forms of freedom are very limited in their practicality and that Christianity seeks to offer a higher and more practical form of freedom.

Existence Precedes Essence

The phrase "existence precedes essence" is defining of existentialism, especially the form it took under Jean-Paul Sartre in the 1950s. Interestingly, despite never living to see postmodern existentialism become a formal philosophy, Chesterton captures this existentialist principle in similar language, challenging the notion that "matter precedes mind." He claims, "If we want to uproot inherent cruelties or lift up lost populations we cannot do it with the scientific theory that matter precedes mind; we can do it with the supernatural theory that mind precedes matter."[7] For Chesterton, "mind precedes matter"—and its equivalent, "essence precedes existence"—is the "supernatural theory" that is more at home in Christianity, because it presumes a dignity and purpose that is already given and determined before one even exists. On the contrary, the existentialist quest is to *create*

---

7. Chesterton, 143.

purpose in this life rather than to *find* meaning already established by an external authority. The irony in using the word "quest" for creating meaning lies in the aforementioned principle that one cannot make his own adventures: "For an adventure is, by its nature, a thing that comes to us. It is a thing that chooses us, not a thing that we choose."[8]

Chesterton distinguishes the "scientific theory" from the "supernatural theory," and he rightfully traces "matter precedes mind" to the former and the inverse to the latter. Just as many determinist arguments tend to confound science and philosophy, we see the confounding of science and philosophy now in existentialism. Science, in treating the material world, will naturally conclude that "matter precedes mind," but this material explanation must *not* be applied philosophically to the realm of meaning, the nature of being, and the transcendent. Metaphysics, not physics—philosophy, not science—studies being *qua* being.

Individualism

Given the emphasis on personal freedom and a personal creation of meaning, it is no surprise that individualism is both a principle and expression of existentialism. In addition to all that was just said about freedom and creation of meaning, the individualistic forms of freedom tend to reinforce individualism. Other individuals can often pose themselves as threats to one's own freedom, if freedom is understood to be the absence of restraint and the power of choice. Because others can limit one's own options and restrain him from carrying out his own desires, he must react by asserting his own good over that of others.

Existentialism often appeals to personal rights as an expression of individualism. Rights are concerned with protecting one's own freedom. Although some rights are inherent to Christianity, the language of rights is often applied to every aspect of life,

8. Chesterton, *Heretics*, 142.

conveying more of a sense of selfish demand than protection of freedom. Chesterton noticed this prevalent language of rights in his time, and we can certainly recognize these assertions around us today: "A whole generation has been taught to talk nonsense at the top of its voice about having 'a right to life' and 'a right to experience' and 'a right to happiness,'" asserting that they are "free" to do whatever they want.[9] Chesterton would like for those people who are claiming universal rights to consider "where their rights came from."[10]

Subjectivism

Again, it is no surprise that the three previous tenets of existentialism lead naturally to subjectivism. With each individual determining for himself or herself what is a meaningful life and what is moral, the common language and principles regarding meaning and morality disintegrate into relativist theories with little relevance to one another. Big systems of principles—especially those heavily doctrinal religious systems like Catholicism—are perceived as threats to the personal quest of creating meaning. Any person or any system claiming, "We have the answer; we found the universal truth," is to be condemned for whitewashing individuality and killing adventure with an oppressive systemization of principles. Organized religion is too all-explaining for the existentialist. The motto of subjectivism rings forth: "The golden rule is that there is no golden rule."[11]

Since each is entitled to his own beliefs, subjectivism has given rise to a culture of avoiding offense. In order to respect the decisions that an individual has made, we leave him alone in order to not challenge the views that he came to. Whatever strange philosophy or religion one holds or does not hold, we

9. Chesterton, *Autobiography*, 324–325.
10. Chesterton, 324–325.
11. Chesterton, *Heretics*, 40.

leave everyone to fashion meaning as suits him or her. "We do not think it matters whether a man is a pessimist or an optimist, a Cartesian or a Hegelian, a materialist or a spiritualist," as if any person's beliefs are just as valid as the next person's.[12] Rightfully so, Chesterton is deeply concerned about the objectivity of meaning, morality, and truth. One's worldview matters much more than we may realize, and one's beliefs are not simply as good as another's.

PROBLEMS WITH EXISTENTIALISM
Impractical Forms of Freedom

The individualistic and relativistic strains of existentialism are huge threats to the objective elements of life. The disintegration of objectivity into subjectivity is apparent in the two aforementioned forms of freedom—absence of restraint and power of choice. Some people imagine that an ideal world would be one where a person could carry out his desires without restraints and have an infinitude of options always open to choose from. However, in practice, we are never without restraint on our choices. Our circumstances, physical health, financial situation, relationships, emotions, and civil law—all of these are conditions to our choices. As for power of choice, one cannot simultaneously choose and keep options open, because "every act of will is an act of self-limitation. To desire action is to desire limitation. In that sense every act is an act of self-sacrifice. When you choose anything, you reject everything else."[13] Rather than preserving freedom by keeping options open, the freedom to commit is jeopardized, and the will is debilitated in the process.[14]

12. Chesterton, 40.
13. Chesterton, *Orthodoxy*, 35.
14. Chesterton, 38–39.

Arbitrary Connections

Since meaning is not to be found but created, according to existentialism, establishing meaningful connections between things and making objects and activities meaningful is the full responsibility of the individual. No external agent has charged creation with meaning; rather, one must create meaning where otherwise meaning would be absent. In choosing one way of life among hundreds, the existentialist expects no one way of life to be more meaningful than another, but one way of life may become more meaningful to the extent that he makes it more meaningful. What this creation of meaning often turns into is a justification of meaning in anything and everything. Without an objective standard of meaning or morality, dull activities and even depraved lifestyles can become justified as meaningful for a person. For instance, a person may justify his habit of pornography as a meaningful activity because, in his mind, it makes him happy and harms no one in the process. In practice, the self-creation of meaning can quickly devolve into forcing meaning into activities, lifestyles, and objects. A time may come when one realizes that he has been making meaningless connections for years. Making connections between created things must involve an external criterion against which to judge what is objectively meaningful.[15] For Christians, God himself is the arbiter who has provided an objective scale of meaning to direct humans toward an objectively meaningful life, one that can be judged according to a standard.

Search for Its Own Sake

One way in which existentialism undermines the objectivity of meaning is treating life as a search for its own sake. Existentialism, like mythology in Chesterton's treatment of it in *The*

---

15. Duncan Reyburn, *Seeing Things as They Are: G.K. Chesterton and the Drama of Meaning* (Eugene, OR: Cascade Books, 2016), 101.

Everlasting Man, is a "search" for meaning.[16] The fatal problem with the existential search, however, is that it does not know what it is searching for. Inherent to existentialism is the principle that personal meaning does not exist apart from the meaning one creates. An answer has not been given except the one that a person must create to make this life meaningful. But as soon as an answer exists, the questioning is over; the thrill of the search has come to an end, so it may seem. Rather than killing the prey and enjoying the kill, one may prefer to prolong the hunt so as to perpetuate the thrill of the chase. The search for truth is preferred over the truth itself, which never comes to be possessed.

One form that this search for its own sake takes is always looking forward, never backward, for an answer. Because anticipation of an answer bears a sense of thrill, we can tend to deny that an answer has already been given, and we tirelessly look out for answers and set our hopes for happiness on promises, like the cure for cancer, a new philosophy better than the rest, an end to death, groundbreaking technology, a new lifestyle that will fill us with happiness, and so on. But the search for its own sake never fully satisfies: "Now when people merely plunge from crush to crush, and from crowd to crowd, they never discover the positive joy of life. They are like men always hungry, because their food never digests; also, like those men, they are cross."[17]

For Christians, however, an answer has already been given in Christ. In the midst of the mythological search, which existentialism has carried forth into postmodern times, Christians look to the past in glad termination of the search, which is more rightly called a wandering. Christians know that "the best things that happen to us are those we get out of what has already

16. G.K. Chesterton, *The Everlasting Man*, in *The Everlasting Man: A Guide to G.K. Chesterton's Masterpiece*, ed. Dale Ahlquist (Elk Grove Village, IL: Word on Fire, 2023), 174.

17. G.K. Chesterton, *The Well and the Shallows*, in *The Collected Works*, 3:413.

happened."[18] Interestingly, the answer that an individual finds in the past moments of his own life and in the past events of Christian history is not the end of the search as much as it is a conditioning of it. Knowing what to look for does not diminish the thrills and surprises that will occur along the interrogative process. An objective answer is given in Christ, and we can journey through the uncertainties of life guided by this answer. Likewise, an objective answer is given in one's objective purpose, and the Christian seeks to order the details of the unfolding story according to this answer. The entirety of one's purpose is never fully revealed, but the promises of the past are guiding lights for the unfolding future through which one's purpose is gradually elucidated.

Objectivity and Subjectivity Undermined

The previous examples have suggested that existentialism can undermine objectivity if meaning is defined and fashioned on everyone's own terms. Unlicensed subjectivism threatens the unity of the whole story of creation, in which every person, even with his or her own uniqueness, is united by an objective factor or reference point. The objective factor and reference point is God himself, and whatever unity is achieved at the end of time will be due to every soul being connected through God, apart from whom no unity is ultimately achievable. With the denial of God or of objective truth, one's connectedness with others is severed due to the lack of an agreed-upon standard.

Interestingly, existentialism can be said to threaten the subjectivity, in addition to the objectivity, of the grand story. Individualism ironically whitewashes and flattens one's individuality, that is, one's uniqueness intentionally chosen by God.[19] By shirking the meaning and the purpose bestowed upon an individual

18. Chesterton, 413.
19. Chesterton, *Autobiography*, 35.

individual by virtue of existing, one loses the unique self and unique adventure of life prepared by divine choice in preference for a duller self and duller adventure concocted by human choice. It is as if one were asked to perform a certain role in a play and instead invented new lines and performed unconventional actions that clashed with the intended narrative. In God's play, creativity is encouraged and promoted in the performance of one's unique role. Authentic self-expression not only is liberating but also incorporates one into a much grander story.

Living One Hundred Lives

Deep down lies a desire that our existence achieve both perpetuation and integrity. Meaning is correlated with duration, it can be argued. We see this when people name what a meaningful life will have been by the end of life—leaving a legacy, making a positive impact that will ripple down for generations, being established in the memory of human history, or perpetuating the family name through children and grandchildren. Arguably the biggest threat to meaning is death, a universally experienced termination of this short experience we call life. Faith in the afterlife is rooted in a hope that this life, far from being rendered meaningless by death, is meaningful in so far as it is perpetuated.

Now speaking to the second and related desire for integrity, just as we desire for this earthly existence to be one with our heavenly existence, we desire that this earthly existence be a unified whole, with past, present, and future bearing relevance to one another. Chesterton describes this deep-seated desire that our life be one continuous story, not a series of unrelated stories:

> He feels that he must have a life, and not a series of lives. He would rather the human drama were a tragedy than that it were a series of Music-hall Turns and Potted Plays. A man wishes to save the souls of all the men he has been: of the dirty little schoolboy; of the doubtful and morbid youth; of

the lover; of the husband. Re-incarnation has always seemed
to me a cold creed; because each incarnation must forget the
other. It would be worse still if this short human life were
broken up into yet shorter lives, each of which was in its turn
forgotten.[20]

For Chesterton, there is something ultimately repulsive
about living a disintegrated life of unrelated adventures, even if
the adventures are thrilling as they occur. Each adventure of the
past longs to be further realized in the future, and every adventure of the future longs to bear a connection to the past.

In two other books, Chesterton describes this experience
of disintegration as a nightmare. About a person who tries to
live a hundred different lives, he claims, "The universal vision
of being such a Briareus is a nightmare of nonsense even in the
merely imaginative world; and ends in mere nihilism in
the social world."[21] Chesterton traces this nightmarish spirit of
pluripotency to modernity: "Now, it is this horrible fairy tale
of a man constantly changing into other men that is the soul of
the Decadence. . . . But to that nightmare we give the name
of modern culture."[22]

This spirit of the modern culture is the product of existentialism. With the existentialist understanding of freedom as the
power of choice, the mentality of pluripotency quickly becomes
an experiment of fantasizing about the hundred other lives one
could be living. Even if the true existentialist would call such
scattered yearning "bad faith," such splitting of the will is a necessary result of the existentialist view of freedom. Without the
certainty and objectivity of one's purpose to grant confidence in

20. G.K. Chesterton, *Divorce Versus Democracy*, in *The Collected Works of G.K. Chesterton* (San Francisco: Ignatius, 1987), 4:428–429.

21. G.K. Chesterton, *The Superstition of Divorce*, in *The Collected Works*, 4:289–290.

22. G.K. Chesterton, *The Defendant* (London: J.M. Dent & Sons, 1901), 33–35.

a life decision, one will forever be searching for an answer among a hundred life paths. Questioning one's own life, an individual can become jealous of the lives of those around him, wondering what his life would look like if he were married to his friend's beautiful wife or if he were a lawyer in the UK rather than a doctor in the US. Rather than embodying his own role in God's grand story and promoting the faithfulness of others to their roles, he seeks to live every other role in addition to his own, only to fail to live up to his own role and to take away from the roles of others. As Chesterton puts it:

> He wishes to walk down a hundred roads at once; to sleep in a hundred houses at once; to live a hundred lives at once. . . . He would be an insane sultan jealous of the whole human race, and even of the dead and the unborn. I believe that behind the art and philosophy of our time there is a considerable element of this bottomless ambition and this unnatural hunger. . . . They are crying for the world; and when they had it, they would want another one.[23]

Never satisfied with what has been given, this individual ravenously devours the stories of others, stories that he perceives as his own. According to his pusillanimous perspective, this existence is a one-man play in which he enacts every role, if not in practice then in the fantasies of his mind. He proudly announces his plan to himself, as if failing to notice the irony of his statement: "Let us have the splendour of offering ourselves without the peril of committing ourselves; let us see whether one cannot commit suicide an unlimited number of times."[24] Rushing forth with his plan, he ignores the maxim ringing forth from his heart:

23. Chesterton, *Superstition of Divorce*, 289–290.
24. Chesterton, *Defendant*, 37–38.

169

"For he that lives more lives than one / More deaths than one must die."[25]

Existential Crisis

The ironic truth about existentialism is that it sets up for existential crisis. Deceiving oneself or letting oneself be deceived by others can endure for much of one's life, because what is sought in the lie is not the 1 percent of falsehood but the other 99 percent that is true. But one degree off is all it takes to end in the wrong place down the road. Especially during one's youthful years, the tenets of existentialism appear to comprise a workable philosophy that gets the most out of life. Arbitrary connections, personal creation of meaning, the thrill of the search, the fantasy of a hundred lives—they provide enough stimulation and meaning to postpone the pursuit of deeper meaning, which requires commitment and therefore a more authentic form of freedom— the freedom to commit. But these sources of meaning, however legitimate they may be, are only glimmers of a satisfying answer; they are not the answer itself, which must be complex if it is to satisfy the human heart.

While one's arbitrary assignments of meaning may have sufficed for a while, a time comes when one is "tired of 'pretending.'"[26] The truth-telling instinct that had been quenched down to a tiny ember has reignited. Reviving the faint memory of an objective truth, one frantically wonders whether he had settled for objectively shallow meaning during all these years. His heart is weary of the lie that sin does not exist; the heart rebels because it had to bear the grief and confusion all those years. Although everything had remained in the dark of one's mind and heart for years or decades, the internal disorder suddenly surges up to receive exposure to light and air that it might live again and be

25. Chesterton, 34.
26. Chesterton, *Everlasting Man*, 255.

set right. One's whole past demands an account; the past yearns to be severed no longer from the present and future. One's life demands a just reckoning, "for no one wants to be forgiven for a big sin as if it were a little one."[27] Life has caught up to him; it wants real answers now.

By fabricating answers and meaningful connections but never finding an answer, existentialism, if it does not admit to a satisfying answer, will face the same fate as mythology—"eroticism."[28] An existential crisis is a time of upheaval that offers two options—accepting the objective truth about one's life or continuing to deny the objective truth. In the former case, justice purifies away the falsehood of the past, reintegrates one's entire life into a meaningful whole, and connects one's life to the lives of others. In the latter case, with the denial of an objective answer, one begins to seek "stranger sins" as an escape from the purifying fire of justice.[29] Chesterton names a few of these escape routes as drug addictions and strange cultic practices not far from devil-worship.[30]

THE RESPONSE OF CHRISTIANITY TO EXISTENTIALISM

Affirms Objectivity

The Christian position, as a response to the relativism of existentialism that divides each individual's experience from one another, champions objectivity as the unitive factor. The objectivity of the Christian worldview is many things—the one divine Author of every human story, the one grand story of creation comprised of individuals' stories, and the universal call to joy and holiness affirming union with God as the objective of everyone's life. The objectivity of the Christian worldview does not

---

27. Chesterton, *Orthodoxy*, 97.
28. Chesterton, *Everlasting Man*, 255.
29. Chesterton, 256.
30. Chesterton, 255–256.

threaten subjectivity, as if the two were playing a zero-sum game. Rather, the objectivity grants greater dignity to the subjectivity of one's life. For instance, one's uniqueness is not a product of mere human choice but of divine choice; the almighty God has chosen every good detail of each person's life with much more intentionality than any human could ever achieve. Additionally, the claim about the objectivity of the grand story of creation asserts that each person has a special role to play in this narrative. Countless souls are looking to any one person to live out his or her unique story, because his or her success is also theirs. The objectivity of the Christian worldview is "the cement . . . which can prevent [this existence from] falling to pieces in a debris of individualistic tastes and degrees."[31] An objective principle is necessary to achieve the integration of life that we deeply desire.

A "Best" to Strive For

The result of affirmed objectivity is a "best" to strive after. Unlike existentialism, which looks solely to current personal choices as the origin of meaning, the Christian worldview looks backward to find an ideal "fixed before the foundations of the world" to serve as a guiding principle.[32] For Chesterton, this "ideal" is the bliss of Eden (and ultimately heaven), where humans were in perfect union with God.[33] Having been lost, this perfect union is a deep-seated memory that identifies itself as a goal to be returned to. This perfect union—that is, holiness and beatitude—is the standard against which all meaning might be judged and tested. Progress can be made with the establishment of this standard because souls now have a certain direction to guide them.

The notion of a chosen "best" is a door into gratitude and meaningful action. Christianity affirms against existentialism

31. G.K. Chesterton, *The Thing: Why I Am a Catholic*, in *The Collected Works*, 3:156.

32. Chesterton, *Orthodoxy*, 109.

33. Chesterton, 109.

that "mind precedes matter" or, stated differently, that essence precedes existence.[34] The principle underlying these claims is that God had the "mind" and "essence" of individuals in his own mind before their existence. God is not wasteful or superfluous with the details of our lives; he intentionally chose them to contribute to the grand story of creation. Since God is most good and desires that every chosen detail be ordered toward the good of the world, we can trust that the chosen purpose of our lives is for the best of ourselves and others. If God's desire were not the objectively best, perhaps the existentialist preference for personally creating meaning would be superior to the Christian preference for receiving meaning from God. But since God is most good, the pressure to fashion the most meaningful life is relieved, because God desires this more than we do and is more capable of bringing it about than we are. Rather than suppressing the thrilling search for meaning, the Christian worldview enhances the search by preventing us from wasting our time in meaningless abysses and capacitating us for meaning that will last an eternity due to its divine source.

Freedom to Commit

In response to the existentialist forms of freedom—absence of restraint, the power of choice, and the capacity to create values and meaning to one's liking—Christianity offers a higher and more authentic form of freedom: the freedom to commit. Interestingly, for Chesterton this freedom to make a choice is at once an act of "self-limitation" and a "creative power in the will as well as in the mind."[35] It would not be a contradiction to associate limitation with creation. The contradiction that the existentialist sees might result from the understanding of human freedom as a creative power of primary causality, which would mean that

34. Chesterton, 143.
35. Chesterton, *Superstition of Divorce*, 289–290.

humans have the power and the right to create meaning *ex nihilo*, "from nothing." The flaw in this understanding is that only God creates *ex nihilo*. The creative power of free will that we share with God is of secondary causality—namely, the power to freely *order* what has already been created. To this point, Christianity sees existentialism going wrong from the beginning if it carries forth its principle that we create meaning independent from God.

Having revisited this distinction, we might now better understand why Chesterton refers to free choice as both limitation and creation. Free choice is "creative" in the sense that it is the capacity for freely ordering. For Christians, meaning is a product of proper ordering aligned to objective values, not of individualistically creating meaning as if we, independent from God and one another, determined what is meaningful for us alone. Ordering is meaningful because it establishes connections between things in a way that is authentically—that is, objectively—meaningful. Connections that are long-lasting tend to be more meaningful than short ones, but a long-lasting connection requires commitment and authenticity of the meaning behind it. A key example for Chesterton of a meaningful connection is the vow; it keeps one committed, it preserves the authentic life that was vowed to be protected, and it allows more connections to spring forth from its constancy and truthfulness. We might also offer the example of family as a long-lasting connection that is authentic due to its givenness, becoming deeply meaningful due to the high degree of commitment required.

Far from being dull individuals, the saints were those who freely committed to the one life given to them, and their lives were fruitful and meaningful as a result. Chesterton depicts Joan of Arc as a more capacious and complex individual than Tolstoy and Nietzsche because she freely committed to the one life given to her:

Joan of Arc was not stuck at the cross-roads, either by rejecting all the paths like Tolstoy, or by accepting them all like
Nietzsche. She chose a path, and went down it like a thun-
derbolt. Yet Joan, when I came to think of her, had in her
all that was true either in Tolstoy or Nietzsche. . . . She beat
them both at their own antagonistic ideals; she was more gentle than the one, more violent than the other. Yet she was a
perfectly practical person who did something, while they are
wild speculators who do nothing.[36]

Joan of Arc did not regret the other ninety-nine ways of life she
did not get to live; she limited herself to one path and rushed
forth with the freedom of actually desiring to go down that one
path. She would be strangely more capable of the contradictory
ideals of gentleness and violence, because these ideals achieved
their connectedness in God.

Likewise, Chesterton's description of St. Francis echoes his
comments on the integrity of St. Joan of Arc. He says of Francis,
"But after all, this man was a man and not half a dozen men."[37]
Like Joan of Arc, Francis was an individual who left behind the
crossroads to commit to the one life God had in store for him.
He exhibited "the consistency of a complete character" despite
any appearance of inconstancy.[38] What appeared like inconstan-
cies in Francis and Joan of Arc were the complexities of their
character, which commitment to a single noble path draws forth.
All of the saints know what their lives are about, and they are
brilliantly adept at being their full selves.

36. Chesterton, *Orthodoxy*, 39–40.
37. G.K. Chesterton, *St. Francis of Assisi*, in *The Collected Works*, 2:27–28.
38. Chesterton, 27–28.

The Vow

As Chesterton saw it, the vow is quite truly the safeguard and cultivator of romance, story, meaning, free will, and adventure—everything that is true, beautiful, and good about the Christian worldview. Every one of these elements is named in this passage about the vow (certainly not the only words Chesterton has to say about the vow):

> The idea, or at any rate the ideal, of the thing called a vow is fairly obvious. It is to combine the *fixity* that goes with *finality* with the self-respect that only goes with *freedom*. The man is a slave who is his own master, and a king who is his own ancestor. For all kinds of social purposes he has the calculable orbit of the man in the caste or the servile state; but in the *story* of his own soul he is still pursuing, at great peril, his own *adventure*.[39]

In many ways, the vow is a natural expression of the key paradox of meaning. Applying the ideas from the above passage to the key paradox, the vow grants the objectivity of "fixity" and "finality" to frame one's life story, which paradoxically enhances, rather than suppresses, the subjectivity of "freedom." The vow does not eliminate adventure; danger does not disappear at the making of a vow, and the story can still end poorly as a result of disobedience. The vow conditions the adventure, providing weapons and armor against fickle moods and worldly narratives. Far more than a simple suggestion, Chesterton rightly calls the vow an "ideal," and it is difficult to imagine faithfulness to one's story apart from some element of promised commitment.

As already hinted at, the vow is the quintessence of romance in all of its expressions—adventure, fighting and loving, chivalry, and thrift. The finality of the vow conveys the sense of thrift

39. Chesterton, *Superstition of Divorce*, 267–268 (emphasis added).

and limits, "for to be entirely romantic a thing must be irrevocable."[40] The vow would not be a vow if it were revocable and
conditional. Moreover, the vow, being a "fight . . . with oneself"
and bearing "the touch of the heroic," conveys the sense of the
battle for the good of one's soul.[41] Not just a fight for oneself,
the vow is also a fight for the one who is loved. The vow
expresses the positive quality of chivalry, in which the man and
the woman see a dignity in each other that is worth promising
the rest of their lives to protecting and sharing. Vowing is
adventurous because real consequences exist for faithfulness
or unfaithfulness: "Now betting and such sports are only the
stunted and twisted shapes of the original instinct of man for
adventure and romance. . . . If I vow to be faithful I must be
cursed when I am unfaithful, or there is no fun in vowing."[42]
Thus, the vow protects and cultivates romance in all of its forms.

The vow protects and empowers the freedom to commit.
In making a vow to protect something good, the decision made
is "at once free and final."[43] The finality of this promise, rather
than barring one from meaning outside the limits of the promise, allows one to be more free to discover meaning within these
limits. This interpretation is possible if we understand meaning
as correlated with proper ordering, as previously discussed; the
vow allows one to actively order life in a meaningful way when
otherwise it would remain more prone to disorder. One cannot
be fully committed to a single way of life if opportunities remain
open to escape to other ways of life. He must eliminate any
cowardly retreat tactics by "burning his ships," preventing any
future escape from the harbor for when fear strikes.[44] Protecting
his life from devolving into a series of random and unrelated

40. Chesterton, *Heretics*, 56.
41. Chesterton, *Superstition of Divorce*, 233–234.
42. Chesterton, *Orthodoxy*, 123.
43. Chesterton, *Superstition of Divorce*, 267.
44. Chesterton, *Defendant*, 39.

periods of committing and giving up, the vow orders one's life toward eternity, allowing "a moment of immortality" of the past to bear relevance upon one's existence forever.[45]

Survival of Mood

If an objective standard for a meaningful life is not granted, mood can easily become the driver for what is meaningful at different points in our lives. For good reason, it may seem unreasonable to promise our lives to a certain lifestyle when we cannot speak for how we will feel a few years from now, being aware that currently we are "never in the same mood for ten minutes together."[46] Although this reservation begins rooted in prudence, the refusal to commit to one lifestyle ends in never achieving excellence in any one thing. In a sort of laughable but enlightening scenario, we can see the tragic effects that following the mood bears upon one's life: "A man cannot choose a profession; because, long before he has qualified as an architect, he may have mystically changed into an aviator, or been convulsed in rapid succession by the emotions of a ticket-collector, a trombone-player and a professional harpooner of whales."[47] Religious or not, a healthy society requires that individuals get past their changing moods in order to achieve excellence in a certain lifestyle.

The fickle nature of mood is inevitable, and it requires a freely made decision to protect the good against it. For Chesterton, this "free and final" decision is the vow.[48] Chesterton offers the principle that the good can only be reached by enduring a period of monotony or clashing passions: "In everything worth having, even in every pleasure, there is a point of pain or tedium that

---

45. Chesterton, 35.
46. Chesterton, *The Well and the Shallows*, 397–399.
47. Chesterton, 397–399.
48. Chesterton, *Superstition of Divorce*, 267.

must be survived, so that the pleasure may revive and endure."[49] He is right in suggesting that it is the noblest goods in life that demand commitment, from parenting a child to cultivating lifetime friendships. But throughout life these noblest goods are besieged by violent passions, alternative narratives, and enslaving vices. The chief enemy is the devil, who most often works within us to twist our good intentions, obscure the big picture, instill discouragement, and arouse violent passions that disintegrate the coherence of our story. For Chesterton, the Christian doctrine of the fall affirms that man, despite being "the image of God, the wonder of the world and the paragon of animals . . . is not to be trusted."[50] Even the most virtuous person is capable of great evil. This propensity for sin is why the vow is a natural and beautiful expression of the prayer "Prevent us, O Lord, in all our doings," which Chesterton perceives as strong justification for the marriage vow.[51] Knowing our own capacity for ruining our life stories, we pray this prayer to the divine Author, imploring him to rescue our freedom from changing moods and to reorder it toward a commitment to excellence.

49. G.K. Chesterton, *What's Wrong with the World*, in *The Collected Works*, 4:69–70.

50. Chesterton, *The Well and the Shallows*, 365.

51. Chesterton, *Orthodoxy*, 122.

CHAPTER 10

Skepticism

Doubt of the Fundamentals

"One can find no meanings in a jungle of scepticism; but the man will find more and more meanings who walks through a forest of doctrine and design. Here everything has a story tied to its tail, like the tools or pictures in my father's house; for it is my father's house."[1]

TENETS OF SKEPTICISM
Empirical Evidence

While determinist and existentialist tendencies could be said to ebb and flow over the centuries, skepticism, it can be argued, has occupied the arena of faith and reason ever since the Enlightenment. The Enlightenment, represented by figures such as John Locke, David Hume, and Immanuel Kant, among many others, presented a new high standard for truth: truth is correlated with either logical certainties proven by reason or empirical evidence provided by science. From that point of history until today, Catholicism has been on the defense against skeptics who demand that the religious tradition delineate precise evidence for its doctrines, such as the Trinity and the Eucharist. The Catholic intellectual giants of the past few centuries, such as Blaise Pascal, John Henry Newman, and G.K. Chesterton, have taken up the defensive role of apologetics to show the harmony of faith and

---

1. G.K. Chesterton, *Orthodoxy* (Park Ridge, IL: Word on Fire Classics, 2017), 160–161.

reason. Their task has been to demonstrate the reasonability of Catholicism without reducing faith to reason.

Doubt of Universal Principles

A consequence of the Enlightenment standard for evidence is that very few things can be known for certain because of the supposed inadequacy of evidence. In other words, the objectivity of truth is on the defense in modern times. The more universal the worldview, the higher the standard of evidence becomes to prove its universal application. Something as complex and all-explaining as the Catholic tradition, the "universal philosophy" that lays claim to every facet of existence and connects them together, demands that everything prove it.[2] Chesterton is convinced that indeed "everything proves it," but he recognizes the enormity of the task of proving the legitimacy of Catholicism to the skeptic, because everything that exists must be proven as evidence for it.[3] Because larger systems of thought require more evidence, according to the skeptic's process, we can see how the high demand for evidence can quickly become a hindrance to committing to a universal worldview. The skeptic would need to broaden his mind enough to accept the vision that everyone has a purposeful story and that everything proves it.[4]

Doubt of One's Consistent Identity

Just as the skeptic's demand for evidence and logic can undermine the objectivity of truth, the doubt of stability and consistency can undermine the subjectivity of personal identity. This skeptical train of thought might begin with the realization that one's adult self is quite different from one's child self. As a child

2. G.K. Chesterton, *The Well and the Shallows*, in *The Collected Works of G.K. Chesterton* (San Francisco: Ignatius, 1990), 3:391; G.K. Chesterton, *The Catholic Church and Conversion*, in *The Collected Works*, 3:118.

3. Chesterton, *Orthodoxy*, 81.

4. Chesterton, *Catholic Church and Conversion*, 93; Chesterton, *Orthodoxy*, 348.

and as an adult, someone believes very different things, to the point that one doubts whether he is even the same person. Very soon he may think that he is a very different person today than he was yesterday, and that even each moment he is changing because life's experiences are endlessly remolding him. For this skeptic, "there is nothing except change; or nothing except comparison; or nothing except flux."[5] The past bears no relevance to the present, and the present bears no relevance to the future. In light of salvation history, there is no one person to save because flux erases the coherence required for personal identity. Alluding to Chesterton's example of the painting, one's life would be a color perpetually changing hue and tone, ultimately making no enduring contribution to the painting.[6] Changing the metaphor, his life story would be the impossible fairytale of a man who, "swallowed by a whale, might find himself at the top of the Eiffel Tower, or when he was turned into a frog might begin to behave like a flamingo."[7] Salvation, romance, and story require a stable entity upon which to act.

PROBLEMS WITH SKEPTICISM
Shallow Answers

In addition to the problems already hinted at, skepticism can easily become a practice of asking deep questions without reaching deep answers.[8] Skepticism is the victim of its own high standard; this philosophy struggles to reach deep truths because it demands clear evidence and a clean logical process, which it rarely achieves. The result is one we see more often than not in many intellectual circles, which, conditioned by the standard for clear evidence, often cannot provide satisfying answers for the

---

5. G.K. Chesterton, *St. Thomas Aquinas*, in *The Collected Works of G.K. Chesterton* (San Francisco: Ignatius, 1986), 2:530–531.

6. Chesterton, *Orthodoxy*, 114.

7. Chesterton, 123.

8. Chesterton, *The Well and the Shallows*, 387.

probing questions they pose. In treating the ultimate ontological question "What is the meaning of life?" skepticism will cast doubts on historical traditions that have attempted to answer this question in various ways. Skepticism will flirt with different ideas, but in the end it will surrender due to the inadequacy of evidence. Anyone who heeds the doubt-filled whispers of skepticism will feel only farther from an answer.

Paralysis

Skepticism can cast doubt on even the practical aspects of life, leaving one paralyzed in impracticality. By accepting the high standard of evidence as a criterion by which to judge truthfulness of beliefs, one may soon realize that he has little evidence for everything he believes. He is afraid that he has been deceiving himself his whole life. He will ask himself whether he has enough evidence that God exists, that he made the right decision about the woman he married, that he actually exists and is not simply dreaming. Very soon his "whole mood is stricken and riddled with cowardice and sterility."[9] In a charged passage about skepticism's debilitation of pragmatism, Chesterton lays charges against those who are too doubtful to act in practical ways:

> If you feel like that, why certainly you will not found families; or found anything else. You will not build houses; you will not make partnerships; you will not in any fashion do the business of the world. . . . But if you are too sceptical to do these things, you must stand out of the way of those who can do them; you must hand over the world to those who believe that the world is workable; to those who believe that men can make houses, make partnerships, make appointments, make promises—and keep them.[10]

9. Chesterton, 397–399.
10. Chesterton, 397–399.

Applying this passage to the idea of story, the grand story of creation suffers when some do not act. In some cases, individuals might need to make up for the inactivity of others. The hope, however, is that every person lives fully into his or her role, one that is unique to each person.

Flux

As already hinted at, the flux of one's self-identity leaves no stable entity to find a place in the grand story of creation. If the self is changing every moment due to the passing of time and the unavoidable interaction with the surrounding world, then one's past, present, and future bear little to no relevance to one another. An unchanging principle must exist in order to unite seemingly disparate aspects of the self throughout time. Chesterton drives home this point: "A fundamental alteration in the standard is one of the things that make thought about the past or future simply impossible."[11] Chesterton perceived that many people were growing tired of this skeptical mess, seeking after "something that will give form to such a chaos."[12] He takes it one step further to suggest that "millions of men are already at least wondering whether this solution is not to be found in the Catholic order and philosophy."[13]

Approaching Nihilism

Tracing the high standard of evidence to its consequences, skepticism can devolve into the conviction that objective answers and meaning do not exist. It is one thing to have reservations about whether we can come to know objective answers in this lifetime; it is another thing to wearily claim that objective answers do not exist. The former represents a healthy form of skepticism that, if

11. Chesterton, *Orthodoxy*, 31.
12. Chesterton, *The Well and the Shallows*, 475–476.
13. Chesterton, 475–476.

184

it begins to doubt for doubt's sake, can easily become the latter claim of nihilism. Chesterton clarifies that fundamental skepticism—that is, casting doubt on every principle and inquiry—would itself be nihilistic, except that most self-proclaimed skeptics are not this fundamentally skeptical.[14] He makes this observation because to doubt everything would be to doubt one's own thought processes, but of course, the skeptic usually does not doubt the very activities of his mind producing these claims. Fundamental skepticism, according to Chesterton, would look like nihilism: "If a man feels that all the movements of his own mind are meaningless, then his mind is meaningless, and he is meaningless; and it does not mean anything to attempt to discover his meaning."[15] Doubt within the search for truth can gradually become doubt of the process and the goal themselves. As an epistemological system, skepticism can only go so far before it contradicts and deconstructs itself.

THE RESPONSE OF CHRISTIANITY TO SKEPTICISM
Certainty and Uncertainty

Being neither irrational nor ultrarational, Christianity acknowledges both the certainty and the uncertainty of life's answers and meaning. Christianity provides the same answer to skepticism as it did to determinism and existentialism; it draws upon the key paradox that life's meaning is both fixed and unfixed, satisfying the "double spiritual need, the need for that mixture of the familiar and the unfamiliar."[16] Existence's meaning is fixed in the sense that an objective standard of meaning has been chosen by God, who created this world with order. Its meaning is unfixed in the sense that mankind, as finite creatures, seeks after

14. Chesterton, *St. Thomas Aquinas*, 516.
15. Chesterton, 516.
16. Chesterton, *Orthodoxy*, 2.

meaning in a way that is not predetermined; free will is effective in shaping future events.

Given this background, the Christian worldview frames the skeptical claim of uncertainty within the subjective and objective framework of this existence. To a large extent, Christianity agrees with skepticism that many things are uncertain. How exactly God will act in our lives is mostly unknown to us. This is not to claim that God is disorderly. He often acts within the order of the world, but he is also sovereign over it. Such uncertainty on our part allows us to be surprised by the gifts he gives and the adventures he invites us on.

The uncertainty of the Christian differs from the skeptic's in the sense that the Christian has a great sense of the objective truth toward which he is questioning. Major Catholic figures, Chesterton points out, were themselves voracious inquirers: "It was people like St. Teresa who reformed; people like Bossuet who challenged; people like Pascal who questioned; people like Suarez who speculated."[17] Uncertainty for them was a challenge toward greater certainty that could indeed be reached.

Perhaps one explanation for uncertainty in this life is that created things are only small glimpses of the unconditioned Creator. Surrounded by finite beings and entities, we only see facets of God, who is Being itself. Following this idea, uncertainty might exist "because what we see is not the fullness of being. . . . Things change because they are not complete; but their reality can only be explained as part of something that is complete. It is God."[18] Skepticism's high standard for proof can lead to the delayed acceptance of the objectivity of existence—God himself—that is necessary to assent to in order to provide direction to the questioning process.

---

17. G.K. Chesterton, *Where All Roads Lead*, in *The Collected Works*, 3:33.
18. Chesterton, *St. Thomas Aquinas*, 530–531.

For Chesterton, it is common sense to accept certainty about some things and to assent to propositions that may not have all the evidence at hand.[19] Chesterton devotes the first chapter of his autobiography to disagreeing with the skepticism of his time. Fittingly called "Hearsay Evidence," the first chapter involves Chesterton's recounting of his childhood, a time of his life that he is able to recount because he is taking on trust what his family has told him about it. He bitingly remarks, "Some of the sceptical methods applied to the world's origin might be applied to my origin, and a grave and earnest enquirer come to the conclusion that I was never born at all. But I prefer to believe that common sense is something that my readers and I have in common."[20] Whether it is accepting the word of another or assenting to the religious tradition handed on to us, Chesterton thinks it practical and commonsensical to accept many things with certainty: "A man who believes something is ready and witty, because he has all his weapons about him. He can apply his test in an instant."[21]

The common sense of believing something allows one to bear fruit. In fact, a useful question for discerning the wise course of action is to ask where the fruit is. Chesterton connects the common sense of Christianity to its fruitfulness: "For it was the soul of Christendom that came forth from the incredible Christ; and the soul of it was common sense. Though we dared not look on His face we could look on His fruits; and by His fruits we should know Him. The fruits are solid and the fruitfulness is much more than a metaphor."[22] When the slew of doubts undermines the practical and discerning spirit within us,

19. John Henry Newman makes a similar argument in *An Essay in Aid of a Grammar of Assent*, which Chesterton most likely read.

20. G.K. Chesterton, *The Autobiography of G.K. Chesterton*, in *The Collected Works of G.K. Chesterton* (San Francisco: Ignatius, 1988), 16:21.

21. G.K. Chesterton, *Heretics*, in *The Collected Works*, 1:65–66.

22. G.K. Chesterton, *The Everlasting Man*, in *The Everlasting Man: A Guide to G.K. Chesterton's Masterpiece*, ed. Dale Ahlquist (Elk Grove Village, IL: Word on Fire, 2023), 459.

we might ask ourselves, "Where is the joy, the peace, the hope, the adventure, and the fruitfulness?" Common sense will show us that the fruitfulness lies in the certain fact of Christ's coming among us and our encounter with him, which, once experienced, cannot be forgotten.

SKEPTICISM TOWARD THE EXISTENCE OF EVIL

As a final consideration, besides the "suicide of thought" that results from skepticism, Chesterton was intensely interested in the modern (and what he considered to be inconsistent) disbelief in the existence of evil, not simply as a subject for theological debate but "a fact as practical as potatoes," which no sane person could deny and which has scarily practical implications for everything.[23] In case one's belief in the fall or theology of good and evil seem to be simply a matter of personal taste or opinion, Chesterton helps us to realize that these views make all the difference for our happiness and sense of meaning in the world. In an extreme case, the difference is between fighting for good in the world or killing oneself because evil appears to have overcome good. Chesterton identified skepticism as a prominent outlook on evil during his time, and other popular positions on evil, including pessimism, optimism, and dualism, were not much better, as we shall see. The proper take on evil is what Chesterton would call "patriotism," which asserts "positive evil as the starting point" and, in identifying the disease, fights to overcome it.[24]

First considering the skeptical approach toward evil, Chesterton had to face the modern tendency to doubt or deny the reality of sin; this tendency is a direct result of dismissing the doctrine of the fall, because now sin and evil go unexplained. It was in *Orthodoxy* that Chesterton had to use the metaphor of

23. Chesterton, *Orthodoxy*, 8.
24. Chesterton, 8.

insanity to illustrate sin, because his contemporaries were "disput[ing] original sin, which is the only part of Christian theology which can really be proved."[25] In *Heretics* Chesterton predicts the failure of H.G. Wells' "Utopia," which required the denial of original sin. He explains, "The weakness of all Utopias is this, that they take the greatest difficulty of man and assume it to be overcome, and then give an elaborate account of the overcoming of the smaller ones."[26] To deny the fall is to treat the greatest cancer of humanity as cured when it is actively consuming and sapping the life of humanity. The denial is an assertion of health when sickness prevails, of fulfillment when the ideal is far off, of victory when the battle is far from over. The first step in overcoming the enemy of humanity's story is to acknowledge that humanity has an enemy; in fact, this enemy has tricked humanity since the beginning into accepting a narrative other than God's best story. The well-known adage that "the greatest trick the devil has done is convincing the world he does not exist" could not be more aptly applied to Chesterton's times.

Second, the pessimistic view of the world is to treat evil as more powerful than it is. According to Chesterton, pessimists "make a plan of life of which the background is black . . . then admit a speck or two of star-dust more or less accidental, or at least in the literal sense insignificant."[27] Good is treated as a sort of mistake; any meaning in life, if it is granted, turns out to be trivial in the end. Death relativizes all meaning and has the final say. Reaching maturity surrounded by this narrative, Chesterton knew these theories could not explain this existence, which "reduced to its most primary limits was extraordinary enough to be exciting."[28] For Chesterton, the theory that was more consistent with experience was the fall, not these dark outlooks on life

25. Chesterton, 8.

26. Chesterton, *Heretics*, 77.

27. Chesterton, *Everlasting Man*, 407.

28. Chesterton, *Autobiography*, 96.

that encouraged giving up on the world: "The old theological theory [of the fall] seemed more or less to fit into experience, while the new and negative theories did not fit into anything, least of all into each other."[29]

Third, the weakness of the optimistic view is that it treats evil as too little of a threat. Contrary to the pessimists, the optimists draft up a vision of the world on "white paper . . . and explain or explain away somehow such dots or smudges as may be difficult to deny."[30] Rather than denying the existence of evil as some would, the optimist admits to a few exceptional cases of evil and suffering but overall views them as rare occasions that do not put a damper on the upward trend of humanity. For the optimist, humanity is progressing and improving by an almost automatic process; evil and suffering might be perceived as soon to be eliminated if they are still in consideration. Despite all the talk of promise and potential, Chesterton judges optimism to be conceivably more grim than pessimism: "On the other hand, something else tells him that it is unmanly and debased and even diseased to minimise evil to a dot or even a blot. He realises that optimism is morbid. It is if possible even more morbid than pessimism."[31] The promise of the optimist is debased in the same way that the offer of a con artist is. The lure of the optimist is freedom from responsibility to use one's free will properly, but this ultimately is an insult to the great gift of freedom that is the door into a life of adventure and thrilling decisions. The optimist claims that no change in one's life is needed; in fact, things are improving. But this is not the reality of life: "Things naturally tend to grow worse. . . . If you leave a white post alone it will soon be a black post."[32] The optimist seems to say, "This is our final destination; we are home." We might imagine Christianity

29. Chesterton, 171.
30. Chesterton, *Everlasting Man*, 407.
31. Chesterton, 407.
32. Chesterton, *Orthodoxy*, 114.

responding, "Beatitude is our final destination; we are not yet home."[33] Christianity's message is not morbid; it is the truth, and it is hopeful. Our true home is faintly visible on the horizon, "and the steepest adventure is to get there."[34]

Fourth, the dualist position, in treating good and evil, might view the fall as caused by an evil being coequal with God. Chesterton offers an image for dualism: "Life is like a chessboard in which [good and evil] are equal, and can as truly be said to consist of white squares on a black board or of black squares on a white board."[35] Chesterton acknowledges that the dualist position is possibly the "easiest of all."[36] Chances are that most people would be quicker to take a dualist position than an optimistic or pessimistic view, because dualism seems more true to experience—life is good much of the time, yet suffering occurs much of the time. This common observation can lead to the dangerous—and heretical—position that evil is just as primary and powerful as good. If this view is followed down to its implications, it suggests that God's grand story of salvation and his story for each individual may not actually reach fulfillment if evil is victorious in the end. Even on a smaller scale, the dualist view can infect the moral life with the suggestion that an evil means can justify a good end, if it is granted that evil has substance. The Christian view, which Chesterton's patriotic view represents, claims that evil can never justify a good end because evil lacks substance; it requires a host to parasitize. One other important clarification is that Chesterton's romance of *St. George and the Dragon*, in its representation of the Christian story, is not dualist. We, embodying the role of St. George, are already victorious over the devil insofar as we actively share in Christ's certain victory over the devil. At the same time, our share in

33. Chesterton, 76–78.
34. Chesterton, 123.
35. Chesterton, *Everlasting Man*, 407.
36. Chesterton, 407.

the victory of Christ is not guaranteed or fated. Though it may appear that evil is a coequal force in the meantime, we are "already but not yet" victorious in Christ, as the Christian faith would express.

The fifth and final position is Chesterton's expression of the Christian position—patriotism. The fundamental principle of patriotism is, as Chesterton wittily puts it, "that right has a right to be right and therefore a right to be there, and wrong has no right to be wrong and therefore no right to be there."[37] What may seem like a simple claim—that good is more primitive than evil—has tremendous implications on life. It saves one from admitting even the smallest bit of evil as inherent to creation because "every existence, as such, is good" inherently.[38] Evil is not meant to exist; or stated as more theologically sound, evil is non-existence or non-substance that is not meant to be in this world. Chesterton provides illuminating language by describing evil as "an enormous exception" and "an invasion or yet more truly a rebellion."[39] What these metaphors rightly capture is that evil is contingent upon good, requiring a host to parasitize or an order against which to rebel.

Moreover, the primitiveness of good has important implications for one's life story. While a dualist view of evil may suggest that one's goodness is violable, Christianity asserts that one is made inherently good. Evil cannot violate one's inherent goodness, but it can prevent one from living into its fullness. While dualism presents good and evil as equal options, Christianity asserts that evil is never a viable option, even if it attempts to present itself as such. The inherent goodness is for Chesterton a romance of recovery, finely expressed by the novel *Robinson Crusoe*. Just as Crusoe salvaged and treasured only a few items

37. Chesterton, 407.
38. Chesterton, 407.
39. Chesterton, 407.

from a shipwreck, inherent goodness is experienced more as a "relic to be guarded" than the original ship in its fullness.[40]

This romance of recovery conveys many key points of patriotism. For one, patriotism names evil for what it is and fights against it to recover the primitive good. Sticking to the shipwreck image, the Christian patriot acknowledges the primeval shipwreck—that is, the fall—knowing that admitting this tragedy will provide a driving force to rebuild the ship and return home. Still stranded on the island, the patriot firmly declares that this small island, though good in the limited things it has, is not his true home. The stranded sailors possess relics of their true home that they saved from the ship, reminding them to labor with hope for their homecoming. Not leaving the island to ruin, the patriot loves what is good on the island, using its materials to rebuild the ship and treating the island as home in the meantime. For Chesterton, this is a fitting explanation for "why [he] could feel homesick at home."[41]

One final point about the fall is that Chesterton views this primordial event as one of a larger Christian story that best explains our reality. As already observed in the many stances on good and evil, problems arise when giving evil too much or too little credit. While pessimism, optimism, dualism, and a denial of evil leave one ultimately dissatisfied with their explanations of the human experience, Christian patriotism presents a story that is "like life":

> . . . that strange story of treason in heaven and the great desertion by which evil damaged and tried to destroy a cosmos that it could not create. It is a very strange story and its proportions and its lines and colours are as arbitrary and absolute as the artistic composition of a picture. . . . But that

40. Chesterton, *Orthodoxy*, 78.
41. Chesterton, 78.

strange story has one small advantage over the diagrams. It is like life.[42]

For Chesterton, the story of the fall is a "strange story" about an enemy who is not coequal with good because he "could not create" like God; he could only "damage" the world. Though the primordial desertion was not the will of God, the story is "strange" in that strong elements of God's will and evil's will can be perceived in it. God's picture had intentional detail and proportion even before the fall, and the story could be written without evil, as evident in Chesterton's play *The Surprise*. Even then, God allows for his highest angels to desert him out of free will. Somehow the will of evil finds a place in God's story, yet it will not have the final say in the story. The principles of this Christian story—that God respects free will even when it goes wrong, that evil is contingent upon the existence of good and subordinate to it, and that God maintains the integrity of his story despite (or even by reworking) evil—these are what Chesterton claims to be more "like life" than the other theories of his time. How one interprets the fall can bear greatly upon how one views the role of evil in one's own life story, while the skeptical denial of evil would cast just as much doubt on the story's resolution as it does on the central conflict.

42. Chesterton, *Everlasting Man*, 408.

CHAPTER 11

Nihilism

The Fallout of Inadequate Worldviews

"And its despair is this, that it does not really believe that there is any meaning in the universe; therefore it cannot hope to find any romance; its romances will have no plots. A man cannot expect any adventures in the land of anarchy. But a man can expect any number of adventures if he goes travelling in the land of authority."[1]

NIHILISM

The fourth philosophical position, one that is the natural destination of any inadequate worldview that does not correct its course, is nihilism, the worldview of "despair . . . that there is any meaning in the universe."[2] As Chesterton keenly points out, the despair of nihilism lies not so much in the burden of life's sufferings as in the inability to receive the good. The nihilist has grown "weary of joy."[3] All that he once found meaningful and good—relationships, hobbies, food, the supernatural—turns out to be meaningless to him. Nihilism has struck society "when its food does not feed, when its cures do not cure, when its blessings refuse to bless."[4] Every single philosophy, Chesterton argues,

---

1. G.K. Chesterton, *Orthodoxy* (Park Ridge, IL: Word on Fire Classics, 2017), 160.

2. Chesterton, 160.

3. G.K. Chesterton, *The Everlasting Man*, in *The Everlasting Man: A Guide to G.K. Chesterton's Masterpiece*, ed. Dale Ahlquist (Elk Grove Village, IL: Word on Fire, 2023), 246.

4. Chesterton, 246.

must solve this problem of continuously stimulating man's capacity for meaning, of maintaining his ability "to enjoy enjoyment."[5] Any philosophy that goes about this task in an insufficient or fraudulent way is on its way to nihilism, as we will see.

NEED FOR THE BEST WORLDVIEW

In considering any worldview on meaning, we would be prudent to ask ourselves, "If I hold this philosophy's principles about meaning, where will I ultimately end up?" This is a teleological question, concerned with not only a philosophy's proximate answers but also its ultimate solutions. Many philosophies provide satisfying answers that sound good on paper, but they often fail to explain this complex existence in a large and practical way.

In asking ourselves the above question, we are essentially inquiring which worldview is most true to reality. The human heart wants nothing less than the pure truth; partial explanations will not suffice long-term. "Which worldview is objectively the *best* fit for this existence?" the heart ponders. Anything less than the full truth and a perfect explanation will lead the heart to despair down the road. Realizing at some point that one's philosophical explanations contain many gaps, one will despair about the meaning that he thought he once found or created. It is a daring claim about the ultimate reality but one necessary to make if the difference is a human being fully alive. Any worldview that inadequately accounts for the meaning of this existence can, and often does, end in nihilism.

One way to test the quality of modern popular philosophies is to see where they end, as was Chesterton's strategy. To forecast the endpoint of any popular philosophy is far more practical than tracking its premises to their conclusions. Chesterton would simply observe these philosophies in the prominent figures of his

---

5. G.K. Chesterton, *The Autobiography of G.K. Chesterton*, in *The Collected Works of G.K. Chesterton* (San Francisco: Ignatius, 1988), 16:323.

time, and their unhappy lives were all the evidence he needed to conclude about the flaws of their worldviews. Whether Swinburne's worldview made Swinburne happy is answered by his own belief "that life is a weary river of which the best we can say is that somewhere it reaches the sea of death."[6] Housman's worldview caused him to wearily ask "why he was waked up to live and how soon he may die and go to sleep again."[7] Surveying all the popular philosophies in his contemporaries, Chesterton saw "the inevitable smash of the philosophies of Schopenhauer and Tolstoy, Nietzsche and Shaw, as clearly as an inevitable railway smash could be seen from a balloon."[8] Chesterton's book *Heretics* is essentially a litany of inadequate worldviews that he perceived in his intellectual contemporaries, including H.G. Wells, Joseph McCabe, Bernard Shaw, and Rudyard Kipling. Chesterton then followed *Heretics* with *Orthodoxy*, in which he provided what he believed to be the right worldview, made not by him but by "God and humanity."[9]

DETERMINISM, EXISTENTIALISM, AND SKEPTICISM

It is apparent how the three aforementioned philosophies—determinism, existentialism, and skepticism—can result in nihilism down the road. On the spectrum of meaning, determinism occupies the extreme of pure objectivity. Any subjective elements are explained away by the fixed order of the world. Proximately, our decisions are reduced to chemical reactions and neuron firings in the brain. Ultimately, life must end a certain way; this belief is often called fate. Meaning, if it exists, is objectively set and unalterable. If we follow the principle of determinism "that

6. G.K. Chesterton, *Where All Roads Lead*, in *The Collected Works of G.K. Chesterton* (San Francisco: Ignatius, 1990), 3:56.

7. Chesterton, 56.

8. Chesterton, *Orthodoxy*, 39.

9. Chesterton, 1.

our minds are merely manufactured by accidental conditions," we will soon reach the conclusion that our thoughts, actions, and movements of the heart "have no ultimate relation to truth at all."[10] Determinism fails to account for so much of life's meaning that results from subjectivity. By tipping the balance all the way toward objectivity, the system loses balance and falls apart into despair.

Existentialism occupies the other extreme of the spectrum— pure subjectivity. Any objectivity is undermined by the relativism of each individual's existence. No system or person can determine what is meaningful for anyone else. Meaning is not inherent in creation; rather, the individual decides and creates meaning. Each individual is pure pluripotency without external directionality. Followed to its conclusions, existentialism leads to the relativization of meaning, since billions of individuals have their own say on what is meaningful. Even the meaning in one's own life becomes relativized by the sheer infinitude of possible lives one could live. Chesterton predicts this worldview's spiral down into nihilism: "The universal vision of being such a Briareus is a nightmare of nonsense even in the merely imaginative world; and ends in mere *nihilism* in the social world."[11]

On the spectrum of meaning, skepticism stands in the middle and refuses to commit to a steadfast position. Skeptics are often doubtful of subjectivity, questioning the stability of their own personal identity. They are also doubtful of objectivity, questioning whether answers can be objectively true. Skepticism can be a gateway to nihilism if it leads to the conclusion that answers cannot be found or do not even exist. Fundamental skepticism, put into practice, ends in nihilism: "If a man feels that all the movements of his own mind are meaningless, then

10. Chesterton, *Autobiography*, 41.

11. G.K. Chesterton, *The Superstition of Divorce*, in *The Collected Works of G.K. Chesterton* (San Francisco: Ignatius, 1987), 4:289–290 (emphasis added).

his mind is meaningless, and he is meaningless; and it does not mean anything to attempt to discover his meaning."[12]

Worldviews that are not entirely true to this reality and are inadequate in their principles are bound to crack when tested against reality. They can work for a while, but not forever. They can explain a lot, but not everything. Or to put it differently, they can explain everything, but not in a large and satisfactory way.

THE SUICIDAL SPIRIT

Perhaps one of the most accurate practical descriptions of the nihilist is Chesterton's description of the suicidal spirit in *Orthodoxy*. The suicidal spirit as it relates to nihilism refers less to the act of taking one's life or the mental disintegration that leads up to that action. Instead, it refers more to a worldview and a way of valuing (or more precisely, devaluing) the world such that even someone who never takes his own life could be guilty of insolently devaluing it. The nihilist, bearing a suicidal spirit, despises the world and carries an air of opposition to everything that exists, including his own life. If he grants the existence of God, then God is a treacherous deity that so hated the world that he created it and brought the nihilist into existence to have to experience it.

The nihilist represents the opposite of Chesterton's notion of patriotism, which is an attitude of loyalty in order to make something or someone better, even if that place or person is not currently in good shape. Like Satan, who is the cosmic anti-patriot, the nihilist is an anti-patriot, valuing nothing as worth fighting for. The nihilist looks outward and inward and feels combative animosity, if not cold indifference, toward all things. And the combative animosity can barely be called defensiveness, for he is not interested in defending himself against another

12. G.K. Chesterton, *St. Thomas Aquinas*, in *The Collected Works*, 2:516.

party. In fact, in its extreme form, the nihilist can hardly be said to be prideful, for he does not even take pride in his identity, his beliefs, or his own existence.

For Chesterton, nihilism is the ultimate offense against heaven and against earth. While all the worldviews Chesterton argued against—whether determinism, existentialism, or skepticism—were dangerous and worth combatting, they at least took a stance on the world and fought to the death to defend it. This is why Chesterton ultimately admired his friend Bernard Shaw despite disagreeing in every respect with his atheism, because Shaw was consistent and persistent in the defense of his worldview. The determinist, the atheist, and the relativist all feel some degree of gratitude to be alive. Even during his darkest years, Chesterton, in the spirit of Christian patriotism, felt deeply that existence was better than nonexistence, that "even mere existence reduced to its most primary limits was extraordinary enough to be exciting."[13] The nihilist, on the other hand, believes that nonexistence is better than existence and wishes that he did not even exist to have to take a position on existence. Nothing on this earth, insofar as he has numbed himself to it, can really save him—not the flowers of the field, nor the laughter of children, nor the offer of wealth and fortune. As Chesterton suggested, the nihilist is beyond bribing, making even a criminal more noble in his desire to achieve a good end, albeit through an evil means.[14]

In this way, nihilism is truly the spirit of hell upon earth. The nihilist joins the army of Satan in proclaiming "Non serviam" and hates his own denial of service in the process. Whether we wanted it or not, God gave every person a life upon their entrance into the world, a story to co-create with God. The story does not exist just for the brief span of a human life but, as the Christian faith would suggest, forever, even after death.

13. Chesterton, *Autobiography*, 96.
14. Chesterton, *Orthodoxy*, 70.

Whether the nihilist believes he exists beyond his earthly life or not, he reflects upon the fragile human experience that he somehow ended up with and bitterly concedes, "What a cruel world, what a trap is the human experience! I never wanted this in the first place." God gives him his own story, but he never wanted a story. God gave him a story to fit into a larger narrative that will be celebrated at the end of time, but he never asked to be invited to the celebration.

Viewing it through the lens of nihilism, hell could be perceived not so much as a united army of angry rebels surrounded by fire and smoke, with Satan at the head and souls aggressively combatting the hosts of heaven. No, more in line with Dante's depiction of the deepest depths of hell in *The Inferno*, the hell of nihilism could very well be frozen over with cold indifference. Nihilism is the preeminent form of the "Suicide of Thought," as Chesterton's chapter in *Orthodoxy* is titled. Any worldview that takes one truth as all-explaining can stop thought and trap one inside a cramped mental headspace of one idea. The determinist and existentialist are interested in knowing "why" when they look around and seek to explain the world. However, the nihilist is not interested in knowing "why" about anything. At the extreme limit, the nihilist has no thoughts and no ultimate relation to anything as far as he is concerned.

Meanwhile, heaven could be said to be the opposite of cold—fully alive with warm mirth and joy, each soul blazing bright with incomparable identity yet in perfect relationship with one another, every intellect yearning to know "why" God intentionally authored the grand story of creation as he did. For while the saints and even Christ himself appeared to many to have been dull and prone to suffering, they shined on earth with divine joy and knew that God was preserving the most sublime experience for the eternal finale.

THE EXISTENTIAL DECISION

It is true that any worldview that does not ultimately align to reality is bound to crack, even if it can work for a while, or explain many things, or persist from generation to generation. However, there inevitably comes that breaking point where the determinist—or any person with an inadequate worldview, for that matter—is tired of pretending that his worldview explains this existence in an existentially satisfying way. To offer what may be an almost too simplistic metaphor, a shirt that is a size too small can be worn for a while but not forever, and sooner or later one will rip it off for lack of it being a comfortable fit.

When this moment comes, one finds himself at an existential decision point. He feels his whole being rebelling against the worldview that he knows cannot work anymore. Two inevitable options arise at this point, and what is not one of those options is to stay the course and hold tight to the inadequate worldview he always had. The only two options are the two extremes: either the worldview corrects itself to be more true to reality, or the worldview doubles down on rebellion and blames existence for the desperate meaninglessness of it all. The former is the road toward the Christian worldview, which welcomes every newcomer with wide-open expanses to run, fresh air to breathe, and a new way of seeing the world, and not just one way among many but the way that the world was always meant to be seen. The latter is the horrific road toward the barren wasteland of nihilism, where the world will make less sense than it formerly did.

The decision point is truly a choice, an election free to make and aided by grace, as God seeks to draw that person toward seeing the world as it was always meant to be. And while the existential decision point may seem to be a dramatic or abstract case of a few individuals on the brink of spiritual and mental destruction, every conversion bears the semblance of this existential event. At a conversion point, one feels that mild continuation of a former life is no longer a viable option; he knows that he must make a fierce commitment to either of two extremes. He will either double down on destruction or have his life turned upside down. What is certain in every instance is that a choice must be made, and the choice bears upon every detail of life, down to one's very happiness.

RESPONSE OF CHRISTIANITY TO NIHILISM

It would not be inaccurate to call Chesterton's life a battle against nihilism—the final result of all the errant philosophies he challenged throughout his life. To the man who knew that one's worldview is the most important thing about a person, nihilism was the ultimate curse of this wonderful existence. The pessimists and optimists of his time sickened Chesterton to his stomach because he saw their ungrateful depression and their insincere happiness, respectively, both leading to the suicidal spirit that gave up on the goodness of this existence. While all of these popular philosophies wore the façade of patriotism to the world's goodness, Chesterton saw his contemporaries one-by-one raising the white flag of surrender. For a while their worldviews attempted to explain this existence, but in the end their inadequate philosophies failed them.

From the beginning of his life until the end, Chesterton battled in defense of meaning. Interestingly, he ends both his autobiography and *Orthodoxy* with similar language, concluding his works and his life where he began as a child. Nihilism, the ultimate end of flawed worldviews, threatened the meaning of this existence, which he found that Christianity sought to protect:

> And its despair is this, that it does not really believe that there is any meaning in the universe; therefore it cannot hope to find any *romance*; its romances will have no *plots*. A man cannot expect any *adventures* in the land of anarchy. But a man can expect any number of adventures if he goes travelling in

the land of authority. One can find no meanings in a jungle of *scepticism*; but the man will find more and more meanings who walks through a forest of doctrine and *design*. Here everything has a *story* tied to its tail, like the tools or pictures in my father's house; for it is my father's house. I end where I began—at the right end. I have entered at last the gate of all good philosophy. I have come into my second childhood.[15]

All of the key themes of Chesterton's worldview are present in this passage. Flawed philosophies end in nihilism because, in some form, they threaten the romance of this life, from adventure to thrift to battle. They undermine the story-like features of this existence, denying the divine Author and his design. Chesterton's life was not disintegrated by simplistic philosophical explanations or paralyzed by doubts. Rather, his life was a romance story with a thrilling plot, with his childhood and adulthood bearing upon each other. Chesterton intuited that Christianity was not playing the zero-sum game of the other philosophies. The objectivity of the Father's design allowed Chesterton to more freely live into the gifted adventures of a story that could have ended in any way. Objectivity and subjectivity, like the lion and lamb, lie down together in the wake of Christianity: "Can the lion lie down with the lamb and still retain his royal ferocity? *That* is the problem the Church attempted; *that* is the miracle she achieved."[16]

As a final point, we might ask ourselves in testing the authenticity of his worldview, "How did Chesterton's life end?" I will speak for myself: That was a man fully alive. That was a great soul. That was a worldview this weary world needs.

15. Chesterton, 160–161 (emphasis added).
16. Chesterton, 97 (emphasis in original).

Conclusion

The purpose of this book has been to present a worldview that best accounts for the objectivity and subjectivity of the human experience. A fitting image has been to visualize major philosophical worldviews as falling somewhere between pure objectivity and pure subjectivity on the spectrum of meaning. What becomes clear in this illustration is that a dialing up toward objectivity is a movement away from subjectivity, and vice versa. Problems arise when life's meaning is treated as a zero-sum game, as many philosophies treat the ontological superstructures of reality. Determinism defends pure objectivity at the expense of subjectivity, and existentialism proclaims subjectivity while precluding objectivity. The Christian tradition has opted out of the zero-sum game in favor of a more capacious explanation for meaning. Characteristic of Chestertonian paradox, Christianity affirms objectivity and subjectivity at their full strength at the same time, accounting for both polarities in such a way that they do not take away from each other.

It turned out that the paradox of objectivity and subjectivity is well exhibited by Chesterton's notions of romance and story. Romance—which for Chesterton means adventure, fighting and loving, chivalry, and thrift—affirms both subjective experience and God's objective purposes. Story—which for Chesterton means art, design, proportion, and an undetermined ending—conveys the subjectivity of the story's course as well as its objective details and ideal ending.

To end this work on a practical note, we might wisely consider what is our worldview on the meaning of life. If Chesterton is right about the effect of our worldview on everything in our lives, then our joy, both present and future, is contingent upon our beliefs. While our principles about the meaning of life may seem a bit abstract, they drive very concrete decisions and viewpoints, where the difference is between waking up each morning with hope or despair, between viewing one's actions as charged with or void of meaning, between finding creation laden with intentional stories or eerily lifeless. This world is either a cosmic mistake devoid of purpose or a grand story overflowing with meaning—the choice is ours to decide what we believe, but one is more "like life," as Chesterton would say, than the other.[1]

As we conclude, we might return to that pivotal question posed earlier: Which worldview *best* explains this existence? I will give Chesterton the final word as he so poetically answers this question for us:

> But in answer to the historical query of why it was accepted and is accepted, I answer for millions of others in my reply; because it fits the lock, because it is like life. It is one among many stories; only it happens to be a true story. It is one among many philosophies; only it happens to be the truth. We accept it; and the ground is solid under our feet and the road is open before us. It does not imprison us in a dream of destiny or a consciousness of the universal delusion. It opens to us not only incredible heavens but what seems to some an equally incredible earth, and makes it credible. This is the sort of truth that is hard to explain because it is a fact; but it

1. G.K. Chesterton, *The Everlasting Man*, in *The Everlasting Man: A Guide to G.K. Chesterton's Masterpiece*, ed. Dale Ahlquist (Elk Grove Village, IL: Word on Fire, 2023), 413.

is a fact to which we can call witnesses. We are Christians and Catholics not because we worship a key, but because we have passed a door; and felt the wind that is the trumpet of liberty blow over the land of the living.[2]

2. Chesterton, 413.

Works Cited

PRIMARY AND SECONDARY SOURCES

Chesterton, G.K. *Appreciation and Criticisms of the Works of Charles Dickens*. In *The Collected Works of G.K. Chesterton*, 15:219–411. San Francisco: Ignatius, 1989.

————. *The Autobiography of G.K. Chesterton*. In *The Collected Works of G.K. Chesterton*, 16:21–331. San Francisco: Ignatius, 1988.

————. *The Blatchford Controversies*. In *The Collected Works of G.K. Chesterton*, 1:373–395. San Francisco: Ignatius, 1986.

————. *The Catholic Church and Conversion*. In *The Collected Works of G.K. Chesterton*, 3:64–124. San Francisco: Ignatius, 1990.

————. *The Defendant*. London: J.M. Dent & Sons, 1901.

————. *Divorce Versus Democracy*. In *The Collected Works of G.K. Chesterton*, 4:421–431. San Francisco: Ignatius, 1987.

————. *The Everlasting Man*. In *The Everlasting Man: A Guide to G.K. Chesterton's Masterpiece*. Edited by Dale Ahlquist. Elk Grove Village, IL: Word on Fire, 2023.

————. *Heretics*. In *The Collected Works of G.K. Chesterton*, 1:39–207. San Francisco: Ignatius, 1986.

————. *The Man Who Was Thursday*. San Francisco: Ignatius, 1999.

————. *Orthodoxy*. Park Ridge, IL: Word on Fire Classics, 2017.

————. *St. Francis of Assisi*. In *The Collected Works of G.K. Chesterton*, 2:25–133. San Francisco: Ignatius, 1986.

————. *St. Thomas Aquinas*. In *The Collected Works of G.K. Chesterton*, 2:419–551. San Francisco: Ignatius, 1986.

————. *The Superstition of Divorce*. In *The Collected Works of G.K. Chesterton*, 4:229–290. San Francisco: Ignatius, 1987.

————. *The Surprise*. In *The Collected Works of G.K. Chesterton*, 11:298–340. San Francisco: Ignatius, 1989.

————. *The Thing: Why I Am a Catholic*. In *The Collected Works of G.K. Chesterton*, 3:135–335. San Francisco: Ignatius, 1990.

————. *The Well and the Shallows*. In *The Collected Works of G.K. Chesterton*, 3:339–533. San Francisco: Ignatius, 1990.

————. *What's Wrong with the World*. In *The Collected Works of G.K. Chesterton*, 4:35–224. San Francisco: Ignatius, 1987.

————. *Where All Roads Lead*. In *The Collected Works of G.K. Chesterton*, 3:27–58. San Francisco: Ignatius, 1990.

————. *Why I Am a Catholic*. In *The Collected Works of G.K. Chesterton*, 3:127–132. San Francisco: Ignatius, 1990.

Reyburn, Duncan. *Seeing Things as They Are: G.K. Chesterton and the Drama of Meaning*. Eugene, OR: Cascade Books, 2016.

ARCHIVES

G.K. Chesterton Collection. University of Notre Dame Rare Books & Special Collections. Notre Dame, IN.

G.K. Chesterton Library. University of Notre Dame London Global Gateway. London, UK.

G.K. Chesterton Papers (1877–1988). Western Manuscripts, British Library. London, UK.